Naming Ourselves, Ourselves, Naming Our Children:

Photo by Alia Almeida Agha

Naming Ourselves, Naming Our Children:

Resolving the Last Name Dilemma

by Sharon Lebell

The Crossing Press, Freedom, California 95019

All of the illustrative accounts presented in this book are based on fact, but I have changed names and circumstances to protect the privacy of the individuals involved, except those involving members of my own family.

Printed in the U.S.A.

Library of Congress Cataloging-in-Publication Data

Lebell, Sharon M.G., 1957-
    Naming ourselves, naming our children

    1. Names, Personal. 2. Patriarchy. I. Title.
CS2389.L43 1988   929.4'2   88-23735
ISBN 0-89594-276-3
ISBN 0-89594-275-5 (pbk.)

To my husband, John Loudon,
my partner in applying the Bilineal Solution;

To our daughters, Kyle and Misha:
May patronymy be passé in their generation.

Thanks to the following people whose influence helped shape this book:

Elaine Gill, my publisher, recognized that last names deeply affect everyone and, as a result, encouraged me to write this book.

Herb Gardner inspired me to consider that names and, by extension, naming systems are not immutable through his screenplay, *A Thousand Clowns*.

Andrea Chesman provided invaluable editorial suggestions, which helped me present my arguments succinctly.

Lyla Grossman taught me to penetrate the cosmetics routinely applied to cultural forms that conceal fundamental absurdities and warrant our scrutiny.

Bernard Grossman proposed—albeit unwittingly—the rudiments of an egalitarian naming scheme, which prefigured the naming system favored in this book.

John Loudon roused me to go public and acted as a sounding board for many of the ideas contained herein.

Una Stannard, pioneer feminist critic of names, wrote a thoroughly researched and deftly argued book, *Mrs Man*, which should be read by anyone who wakes up and realizes that patronymy is obsolete.

Alia Agha, Biaja Teal, Peter Samis, and Barbara Fisher, friskies who think in expansive ways, encouraged me to do the same.

Contents

Contents

The Last Name Dilemma

What's your last name? Where did you get it? Is it your father's? Your husband's? Your former husband's? What about having *your own*? If you are a parent, what last name do your children bear? If you'd like to be a parent, what last name will your children bear? Do you feel that you have the *right* last name? These questions would have seemed preposterous until recently. Not long ago, *The Bay Guardian* in San Francisco chose as its "Ad of the Week" a couple's request for suggestions on what to name their baby:

Help Us Name Our Baby!

Dad has his last name, Mom has hers. What do we name the baby? What did you do? His? Hers? Hyphen? Anagrams? Ideas, please. Write Baby, [address]

Many people are seriously rethinking the way our society traditionally confers last names. There is growing realization that a profound relationship exists between how we're named and how we think of ourselves. Many married women are refusing to live in the shadow of their husbands and no longer assume their husbands' last names. These women are affirming their individuality and autonomy by sticking with their birth names, just as men do. What's more, venturesome parents are questioning the custom of giving children their fathers' last names. There is increasing realization that these

1

two seemingly innocuous customs—married women taking their husbands' names and parents inevitably giving children only their fathers' name—are not appropriate anymore.

We are in the middle of a shift in the way we see ourselves and correspondingly name ourselves. Many socially sensitive people, inspired by an egalitarian ethic and common sense, are in the throes of the last name dilemma. They have observed that traditional ways of naming don't seem sufficiently respectful of female identity and individuality and don't adequately express present-day personal, familial, and social realities.

But those same people experience some uneasiness and ambivalence when considering potential naming alternatives. Only the brave even admit the last name problem exists. And no one, neither the timid nor the bold, seems to know how to resolve it. Those who seemingly would be open to new naming ways are daunted by the challenge of coming up with an egalitarian and practicable way of naming ourselves. To ease their ambivalence, they dismiss the last name dilemma as a low priority on the social agenda.

I'm often asked why I make such a big deal about last names. To most people, a last name is an accomplished fact over which there is no choice. Yet it's clear that the way we are named and the way our children are named is biased. Women usually lose their maiden names when they marry, while men keep theirs for life and pass them on to their offspring. Since childhood I have been vexed by the arbitrary nature of our naming customs.

The time is now ripe for a thoroughgoing assessment of how we name ourselves. I intend to expose the significance of the bias that characterizes how we name ourselves and provide a much-needed, simple and practicable answer to the last name dilemma. I know how eager people are to hear that there is a naming system that embodies present-day values, that respects and remembers female identity and deeds alongside male identity and deeds, that more fully represents humanity and preserves family and human history more inclusively.

The last name question affects *everyone*. Everyone is at some time a child who is named by biological or adoptive parents and has to live, at least for a time, with their birth name. Names are our most intimate symbols, and they are, at the same time, political artifacts. I intend to examine last names through a political lens to see who in our culture is valued, who is not, who is important, who is not, whom we listen to, whom we ignore or silence, who is essential, who is expendable.

For almost two decades there has been a ground swell of experimentation with last names. This movement was in step with the growing concern over the increasingly evident social biases embedded in the English language. Many black people shed last names that originated with slave owners in favor of African names, and thousands of women made up their own last names. Still, even the most clever innovators have yet to come up with a satisfying answer to the question of what to name the children. And there is still a pervasive reluctance, even among generally forward-looking people, to submit the last name dilemma to sustained scrutiny because a solution, though simple in itself, will involve momentous personal and social change. Changing how we name ourselves changes how we identify, rank, and present ourselves to one another; changing how we name ourselves makes us different kinds of people.

Up until now, most of the discussion about new approaches to last names has centered on a married woman's last name and the importance of keeping her own identity. While this is a significant issue, we need to take the broader view and think of naming everyone in a socially responsible way. If there is to be a real change in how females as a group are perceived and treated, there must be a change in how females are named. If women see last names as merely a matter of individual choice, society's view of females as derivative of males or second to males in importance, intelligence, achievement, and ability, won't change.

Though it might appear paradoxical, I don't envision a world in which naming is decreed by law. There are societies today that have such laws, which purport to protect the best interests of the name bearer. For instance, based on a law that went into effect in 1803 under Napoleon, the French still legally regulate first names. In 1987, a French couple gave their daughter a name that was popular in Paris, but unconventional in their rural town. The local prosecuting attorney informed the couple that the name they chose was illegal. Policemen came to the couple's home and seized their family book in which local registrars had inscribed the child's name. The prosecuting attorney ordered the child to be known by her middle name from then on. The possibility of a law similarly enforcing conformity of last names is a nightmarish.

My feeling is that you should be able to make your own choices when it comes to names, though I know from personal experience that it can be hard to go against the prevailing patterns. What's most important is that all people should bear *the right name*, determined by their own criteria, and that each should be free to keep this name for life or to change it as often as they please. But because there is a human tendency to want naming practices to be systematic and expressive of kinship ties, I think the solution to the last name dilemma lies in creating an egalitarian naming system for which there is general consensus.

The Power and the Peril of Our Last Names

Like the color of our eyes, our freckles, the sound of our voices, or the natural talents with which we were born, our names are primary existential facts. We can scarcely imagine our selves separate from our names. Our names act as our ambassadors, traveling to places and times where we ourselves can't be, acting as the representatives of our words, deeds, thoughts, feelings, physical characteristics, and gestures.

Our names are directly linked to the essential something "in" the person for whom they stand. Personal names are the linguistic device we use to evoke and address someone's "whoness." This idea becomes clear if you have ever known someone who changed his or her name. When someone does this, we are suspicious. Why is this person posing, we wonder; you can't change who you are! We are dubious about such name changes because we see the new name as an affectation or a mask.

When I was in the first grade, I had a teacher whose name was Miss Trimble. One day she surprised us by announcing, "Class, I'm thrilled to tell you that my name is now Mrs. Roberts!" The room was silent for several seconds as we digested this. While she expected us to get excited, we were, in fact, aghast; how could Miss Trimble, with whom we felt so familiar, change who she was over a weekend! She falteringly explained that over the past weekend she had married a man named Mr. Roberts. She tried to explain the custom of a woman taking her husband's name upon marriage. Being well-behaved children, we accepted her explanation in the way that children do when they realize that they have to humor adults who do silly things. But, underneath it all, our unedited reaction to her declaration was that it was blasphemous. We, who were ardently attached to our names, to who we were, couldn't conceive of doing such a thing.

As adults, whenever someone we know changes his or her name, we never totally integrate the new name into our understanding of that person. We may oblige that person by using the new name as a functional label, but the new name doesn't truly supersede the old one because an adopted name bears a more remote relationship to a person's true identity than a given name.

At one time I worked for a company with a woman named Dina Carter. During her tenure at this job, she married a man whose last name was Daniels. After she married, she changed the name plaque on her desk to Daniels and in several ways indicated her preference to be called by her husband's last name. We obliged her because it was the courteous thing to do. In our minds and in our conversations at the water cooler when she wasn't there, she was Dina Carter, and she would always be Dina Carter to us. When we had to tell clients that they needed to speak to Dina, we would start to say Dina Carter, but then, in a fraction of a second, we'd effect a switch in our minds to Daniels, and out of our mouths would come "Daniels". To us, "Dina Daniels" stood for "Dina Carter who got married to some guy named Daniels."

Our names are at once intensely private and unavoidably public. To almost the same degree that our names belong to ourselves, they also belong to the people—strangers and intimates—who call us by or know us by a particular name.

Names possess a raw power rooted in our primitive human psychology and recognized in biblical and mystical sources. Many ethnic and religious traditions regard naming as power in its most telescoped form. Names serve their linguistic function of reference by allowing our minds to substitute the name for the actual person. An equivalence is provisionally created for the name and the person, and the apparently disparate ideas of what one's name is and who one is become the same. At this basic cognitive level, a name *is* the thing it stands for. But, at a preconscious level, our minds don't distinguish between the name itself and the person to whom it refers. The name and the person are one and the same. So, when we talk about changing our names, the mind hears that as changing who we are. Names are emotionally and spiritually powerful because we are our names and our names are us. Though our names aren't the only formative influence on our identities, they are primary. So if your name were, say, Teri Jones, you would approach your life as a dramatization of what Teri Jones might or should be like. And your friends and associates would treat you as a Teri Jones might or ought to be treated.

There are countless practices that attest to the collective belief in the power of names. It was the custom among Jews, for instance, to refer to anyone who was sick by a different name in an effort to confuse the Angel of Death. The name Chaim, which means life, was often chosen. When teenagers repeatedly write down the names of those on whom they have crushes, like an incantation, they are showing the close relationship between the beloved's name and the beloved as a person. When we write our names in freshly laid cement in front of our homes, we are trying to announce the fact of our selves, not our names. The recognized power of names, based as it is on the cognitive and spiritual fusion of the self with the name, is sufficient to invest any discussion of last names with great emotion.

Names not only identify us, they also describe us. Both first names and last names dynamically project highly nuanced images that don't lend themselves to easy verbal description. In most cases, it is difficult to discern these images, even while they exert a complex and subtle effect on us. The different images of personal names are powerfully articulate to our preverbal interpretive faculties.

The fact of relationship is universally projected by our last names. First names—in spite of the huge number of, say, Johns or Susans—are mainly to set us apart from others for purposes of identification. Last names, on the other hand, evoke propinquity, relatedness. So even if a last name doesn't outright declare that your father is So-and-So or that you are the husband or wife of So-and-So, in our ordinary social interactions, the fact that you are is one of the essential meanings that is projected by your last name.

One's name is the one clearly manifest characteristic that travels with any individual across a significant period of time. Our names locate us among the social strata; they can proclaim our uniqueness, or render us invisible, hidden behind the mantle of other people's identities. While names themselves are powerful, how we are named, that is, the naming system in which our last names fit, contributes in large measure to the power of our names. Our naming system is *patronymy*.

The Code of Patronymy

It is a symbolic order into which we are born and as we become members of society and begin to enter the meanings which the symbols represent, we also begin to structure the world so that those symbols are seen to be applicable: we enter into the meaning of patriarchal order and then help to give it substance, we help it to come true.

—Dale Spender[1]

Patronymy is the code by which last names are based on fathers' last names. It systematically enforces and conceals one of our culture's basic operational principles: that males are more important than females. An enormous body of beliefs and behaviors radiate from this primary meaning of patronymy. As we apply patronymy's rules, we give its meanings substance, unchallengeable credibility, normalcy, and consequent inevitability. We can't prevent ourselves from deferring to and perpetuating patronymy's unchallenged legitimacy because of its monopoly on the way we generate our names. Even if we don't choose patronymical last names, in the simple act of calling someone by their given or married name we reinforce patronymy, we make patronymy come true.

For whenever we "do" patronymy instead of something else— enact a different way of naming—we not only affirm the propriety of patronymy as a custom, but we also affirm and fortify the meanings it contains. Whenever a woman automatically changes her name at marriage, or whenever a couple automatically names a child by the patronymical code, they are recreating and reinforcing the universal perception that males are more important and therefore superior to females, more deserving, better in every way. We accept, even warmly embrace, patronymy as if it were natural law.

Without exception, all naming codes have to contain biases because of the limited amount of information names can contain and transmit to future generations. When a naming code emphasizes one bit of information, such as the evocation of an ancestor, other information is hidden or cast aside. This highlighting/hiding feature is intrinsic to names and therefore unavoidable. The problem is that patronymy guarantees that male information is highlighted and female information is concealed.

Our culture's adoption of patronymy as its standard naming convention is not accidental or trivial. Patronymy is historically buttressed by the perception of women as chattel. When males first began to consolidate wealth and wished to pass on their holdings to an "authentic" heir, patronymy was used to corroborate paternity symbolically. As an historical reinforcement to patriarchy, patronymy has been a way that the male could put his symbolic seal on kinship groups to establish himself as the dominant member of the group.

At its least, patronymy is obsolete: It doesn't reflect the modern family in its myriad configurations and it fails to represent the true extent to which women determine their own lives and affect the lives of others. At worst, patronymy is insidious in that the precedence of men over women is maintained. Why does it persist?

Patronymy is the product of a set of unstated, yet strictly adhered to, personal and social *contracts*. Like any contract, it consists of a set of provisions and agreements, in this case, ones by which our whole society regulates its behavior and thought. Patronymy's contract, with all of its entailed sub-agreements (the shared assumptions it takes for granted), shows us how patronymy enforces female subordination.

PATRONYMY'S CONTRACT

Main Provisions

I. Males are to have continuous, uninterruptible names, *a name for life*.

II. Females are to have interruptible, serial, provisional names.
    Women are to use their husband's names upon marriage.

III. Children are to be given their father's last name, the patronym, thereby establishing and assuring patrilineality.

Entailments

A. So-called illegitimate children are to be given their mother's last name.

B. The fact of patronymy is not to be discussed so that patronymy's premises and assumptions, including this one, are kept hidden.

C. *Everybody* is to adhere to this contract's rules, and to follow them *without any question or discussion*; i.e., we are discouraged from identifying patronymy in ordinary discussion; moreover, we're forbidden to draw attention to its obvious biases. Most of all, we're *never* allowed to suggest that patronymy might be unjust.

D. Females particularly are forbidden to take a close look at patronymy which could result in their seeing its flaws and implications. Females are, in fact, required to be patronymy's most eager volunteers, cheerful practitioners, and the principal enforcers of all of this contract's provisions. While everyone is required to be patronymy's cops, women are deputized to enforce this contract's provisions through social harassment. Besides maintaining a sunny disposition as they apply patronymy's rules to themselves and their children, females are to regard the provisions of patronymy as special privileges set up on their behalf. They are to pine for the occasions when patronymy's rules are put into effect—on their wedding days and on the days they give birth. Females are to accept patronymy privately and publically; they are not supposed to recognize it as an accident of political circumstances.

E. Males are to relate to the rules of patronymy as a given right. They have the right to keep and pass on their names to future generations. Males are to be pressured by societal sanction to have and to prefer boy children so that their line will be preserved.

F. Everyone is to favor and, if necessary, come to the defense of the male perspective on patronymy. Women are, for example, to understand why they must continue to bear children until they

Some commentary is in order. Regarding the point about women as patronymy's cops, my mother-in-law, Doris Loudon, who is not a member of the Patronymy Enforcement Corps, related a funny but telling incident that happened to her years ago. One day, Doris and her mother-in-law were engaged in a petty disagreement. The anger between them escalated and, in a rage, Doris's mother-in-law shrieked self-righteously, "Just remember, Doris, you're only a Loudon by marriage!" Doris considered the rebuke for a moment, then icily replied, "And what do you think you are!" This episode illustrates the extent to which women embrace patronymy as privilege, but forget the tenuous status of their own names and identities.

While females are required to profess the male perspective on patronymy, males are required to be wholly ignorant of the possibility of the idea of an alternative female perspective. In *Man Made Language*, Dale Spender writes of the sexist bias of language in general:

In my research on language one factor which I have often observed is that while women may appreciate the parameters of male reality, men frequently cannot appreciate the dimensions of female reality. Women "see more"...

Women live under the reality of the dominant group. They are required to "know" it, to operate within it and to defer to its definitions, [to] appreciate the reality of men, for in patriarchal order male reality has usually been posited as the *only* reality. For males, however, the situation is somewhat different.

Men have generated the reality, which women are required to share, and they do not usually have reason to believe that their reality is questionable. This is not just because they can dismiss any alternative meanings which women may offer as "unreal" (or crazy and neurotic) but because women may also collude in preserving the male illusions...

There are occasions when, theoretically at least, it is within women's capacity to enlighten men as to the inaccuracies of some of their definitions, but for numerous (understandable) reasons, women often do not exercise that power. Instead they help to preserve male definitions, to "hide" contrary evidence and to perpetuate the circumscribed vision of many males.[2]

As the contract states, male names are the norm. In fact, within the defining parameters of patronymy, male last names are not only the norm, they are the only kinds of names there are. Dale Spender illuminates this male-as-norm linguistic rule:

One semantic rule which we can see in operation in the language is that of the male-as-norm. At the outset it may appear to be a relatively innocuous rule for classifying the objects and events of the world, but closer examination exposes it as one of the most pervasive and pernicious rules that has been encoded [in our language]. While this rule operates we are required to classify the world on the premise that the standard or normal human being is a male one and when there is but one standard, then those who are not of it are allocated to a category of deviation. Hence our fundamental classification scheme is one which divides humanity not into two equal parts (if two is to be the significant number) but into those who are plus male and those who are minus male.[3]

The male-as-norm rule that is built into patronymy's contract implies that women, whose status is "minus male," are a lesser form of human being compared with males.

That we are to keep silent about the fact of patronymy, as well as its implications, forestalls all possibility of opposition. To recognize patronymy even as a topic of conversation is to violate the implicit assumption that you aren't supposed to talk about patronymy at all. Patronymy demands that it be treated as a foregone conclusion.

As men's names are continuous, their own property, persistent, durable, and *generative* (*i.e.*, they give birth to future instances of their names in subsequent human generations), men's identities are taken for granted as developing in a continuously expansive, unbroken manner. Each man gets to be "his own man" in name and deed; and, strangely enough, a potent generational faculty is attributed to males. On the other hand, women's names are structurally discontinuous, temporary, adaptive, and terminal with respect to heritability.

Female identity is regarded in parallel with female names. As a natural response to the fact of their provisional names and corresponding existential status, women are expected to exhibit malleable personalities, a willingness to adapt to any given situation as an expression of their fundamental discontinuous and dependent names/selves. There is a basic contradiction here. Although women's names are not permanent, it is women who have generative ability. Lest we forget, women are the generative sex.

PERSPECTIVES ON NAMES AND NAMING

Men and those women who have made the unconscious decision to see reality through a male-sympathetic lens have an especially difficult time understanding why there is a problem with patronymy. As is so often the case with a privilege, to those who possess it, the privilege seems like a fact of life, a birthright. Men are the victors claiming the prize, their right to a continuous name and the secondary right of imprinting their name on others. Just as most of us don't regard having ample food on our plates as a privilege, so it is with patronymy for males. The fallacy of privilege, its blind spot, is that those who have it, even those with the awareness that others don't, can't envision a state of affairs wherein they are losers. Those with privilege build a fortress of entitlement around their privilege which gets passed off as natural deservingness.

Patronymy's contract is so powerful, it can be challenging for males to understand the damage that our naming system does to females. I can theoretically explain to males why patronymy poses problems for women, and ultimately for everyone, but most males can't feel it.

In speaking with a man who is married to a woman whose maiden name is Debbie Smith, I can say, "Okay, Harry, how would you like it if your name were Mr. Debbie Smith and all your children automatically became, say, Debbie Smith, Jr., Robin Smith, etc.?" At this point, the male tentatively laughs. On the one hand, the proposed reversal seems so preposterous, so unlike anything in the real world, it's hard for him to take the example seriously. On the other hand, like many men I've talked to, he is laughing because he has perceived a challenge to his naming privilege and is mobilizing his defenses. The favorite argument many so-called progressive men invoke against a challenge to patronymy is, "But isn't patronymy trivial compared with other more pressing women's rights issues?"

Most women who follow patronymy's contract have long ago buried their realization of the injustice done them. Of course, it's very hard for women to face the problems of patronymy— especially if they have already made patronymic naming choices. such as giving their children their husband's last name or taking their husband's name, even "just socially."

There's a flip side to the last name privilege patronymy confers on males. Patronymy poses a burden for men: They bear the onus of carrying on their last names. Not all men wish to have children, and those who wish to may be infertile. They may be subjected to unwanted pressure from their fathers and other family members to create patronymical heirs.

One acquaintance of mine, Sam Winthrop, told his side of the patronymical story, revealing deep anger, sadness, and frustration. Many of his ancestors were famous military men. His last name, Winthrop, is also the name of a fortress which got its name from one of his well-known ancestors. Sam himself had been in the army but became alienated from the military. The rest of his family cherish the association between the name Winthrop and the military that Sam despises. Sam is the oldest of five children. His sisters have married and, by custom, are now using their husbands' names. His brothers have also married but have had only daughters, so the name Winthrop has not been passed on to any of Sam's father's grandchildren. Every time Sam visits his parents, his father berates him for not having children, because it is crucial to Sam's father that there be a Samuel Winthrop V. Sam is made to feel that his value consists only in his ability to pass on the name.

What's wrong with patronymy? The problem can be reduced to one sentence: Males have a name for life, females don't. This simple difference gives males psychological, political, and social advantages over females.

Males and females have different identity development

stories. Males' identities follow a linear path of accretion, an ever-deepening, expanding, and solidifying sense of identity. Females, by contrast, have identity ruptures. They have provisional identities in name and effect. Female names, because of their potential to change are more like labels, while male last names point to an intrinsic core self.

Women's birth names, their so-called maiden names, are quickly forgotten. For instance, at many banks when you open an account, the representative will ask you to supply a bit of information that usually only you would know so you can identify yourself if you lack written documentation. The standard bit of information is your mother's maiden name because, the banks reason, who would know or much care about that?

It is a common mistake to think that the main problems generated by patronymy are personal, as in the case of the woman who wants to retain her own name upon marriage ("I didn't want to lose my identity"). Unfortunately, this focus on the individual woman deflects our attention from the broader social concern of the extent to which women as a group are valued. Such valuing of women's lives will only occur when women gain equal rights to the possession of a continuous name and when women's names have an equal potential for being passed on to future generations. A durable and transmissible name stands for a durable person, someone whose life, words, and deeds make a durable impression on other people and on the annals of history. Whether a name is conferred on a child, a museum, or a monument, passing on one's name commemorates the name and its bearer. Men own their names, women receive them.

Patronymy functions as society's routine endorsement of female expendability. Patronymy encourages us to forget women. We are reduced to nameless wombs, So-and So's wife or mother or daughter. Patronymy predisposes writers of history to forget the fact and facts of women's lives. Patronymy is dangerous for females because *females*, and females only, lose their names. The loss of a name is tantamount to the loss of a person, because we rely on last names to locate and keep track of people.

When a person's name is impermanent, that person's identity is correspondingly provisional. This is very damaging to individual and collective female self-esteem. Males have the luxury of having their last names continuously refer to their implied continuous self. A man may not like his name on aesthetic grounds, but he cannot be alienated from his name. His name and his self are one. Not so for women. Women's names are, and therefore their identities are, a function of whom they were last seen at the altar with. Think of all the women who, because of divorce, walk this earth with the names of men who have become irrelevant to their lives. Consider the countless children who go through life bearing the last name of a biological father who deserted the family before the child ever knew him. Consider, too, the married woman who achieves fame in her own right with her first husband's name and then takes the name of a new husband whose name carries with it no celebrity. It is inconceivable to men to imagine what it would be like to bear the name of someone who is no longer part of their lives.

It is not only women who walk around with derivative identities. Children's names are regularly changed in tandem with their mother's marriages to their stepfathers' last names.

Patronymy also misleads us because it doesn't accurately represent different kinds of families we have today; for example, the blended families that include biological parents, step-parents, step-siblings and half-siblings combined in various ways, or families with one parent. Patronymy is predicated on a father, a mother, and the biological children from their union. All of these individuals are supposed to have the same patronymical last name. But *most* North American families are not configured in this way anymore, and nearly half of the marriages made in America end in divorce.

Since patronymy emphasizes males' names and the corresponding identities of the men who bear and pass on their names to subsequent generations, patronymy skews our judgment of who's important. Conventionally, the patronym is referred to as a family name. Of course, all that really means is that there was some remote male ancestor who, for one accidental circumstance or another, came to bear and pass on that name. Genetically and historically, you are no more like that remote ancestor than you are like all the other ancestors who do not share that name.

Let's look at the mathematics of our backgrounds. Suppose the last name you were given at birth happened to be around ten generations ago, that your great-great-great-great-great-great-great-great-great-grandfather had this name. (This is actually rare. Most names don't survive intact for ten generations.) If you went back to the tenth generation preceding your birth, you would have 1,024 great-great-great-great-great-great-great-great grandparents. Only one great-great, etc.-grandfather among that gang of 1,024 would bear the patronym that was passed on to you. If you were to add up all your direct ancestors (direct ancestors are parents, grandparents, great-grandparents, and so forth, as distinguished from collateral ancestors: cousins, aunts, and uncles) back to that tenth generation, you would come up with 2,046 people. Of those 2,046 people, only ten of them bore (and passed on) this patronym. In other words, more than 200 times as many of your direct ancestors bore another name than the one you happened to get, and none of these other names survive in your name. What's more, we have to remember that of those ten men who represent the line of your patronymical last name, each of them came from, not one line, but two. So, each of those men who bore their given patronym for life did so at the expense of obliterating the hundreds of other names found along their maternal lines.

The point of all this is to illuminate the absurdity of equating a patronymical last name with a family. A patronymical name cannot possibly reflect our varied backgrounds—genetically, historically, or nominally. In view of what the numbers reveal, it is difficult to keep a straight face when someone talks about "So-and-So, who comes from a very old and distinguished family." Who constitutes this old, distinguished family, those ten men out of 2,046 people? What about the 2,036 peasants and dullards who are also part of So-and-so's background?

Maternal generational links, with all the names and corresponding personalities they represent, are generally expunged from our memories. Most people can't reconstruct a maternal line very far back, and this is because female names are purged from documentation of family, social, and world history. Family trees trace a patrilineal path, so while wives and daughters are included in these maps of families, the family names of females are not traced. The result is the suppression of female ethnic background and the spirit and life stories of female members of families. Patrilineal descriptions of families effectively expunge women's identities and contributions. Females are plugged into an artificial patrilineal scheme which confers intergenerational potency on the patronymical family name and on the male family figures, who are seen as the principal actors in their family's historical drama. Patrilineal descriptions of kinship relations are so taken for granted that we forget that they are an arbitrary method of helping us remember our families and who begat whom and who married whom.

Even professional historians and genealogists forget maternal ancestors altogether. A prominent authority on tracing Jewish genealogy and personal history, Arthur Kurzweil, spent years traveling and researching his family genealogy and history. After *seven years* of assiduous efforts, Kurzweil realized that he had altogether neglected his mother's side of the family. So focused was he on his father's last name, Kurzweil, that he didn't realize the huge gap in his intended research. Kurzweil says,

> After seven years of research on one of the many branches of my family, I realized that I had made a mistake: I had neglected all of the other branches. In large part, it was the fact that my last name is Kurzweil which subconsciously made me think that I was more a Kurzweil than a Gottlieb, which is my mother's maiden name. For that matter, I was equally an Ennis, which is my father's mother's maiden name. I am also just as much a Klein, a Loventhal, a Rath, a Grünberg, and countless other names as well. But the fact that we generally take the names of our father, added to the stronger family ties in my father's family, resulted in my becoming singularly obsessed with the Kurzweil family...[4]

When we forget our ancestors, we lose them as a resource for understanding ourselves. When we lose knowledge of our ancestors, we can't even invoke their names to inspire us; those people and what they did and the principles that regulated their lives are not ours to live by and carry on.

It goes without saying that if male names, being transmissible across generations, have higher status than female names, people tend to prefer, consciously or unconsciously, the birth of a boy over a girl. Male children are often preferred over female children because males can give birth to future generations in name, while females cannot. This discontinuity between our naming system and the facts of life is startling.

Under patronymy, women's identities are lost in countless ways. In the canonical texts that deeply influence the lives and behavior of huge religious communities, there is an absurd paucity of women's names, as well as the events of women's lives and their perspectives on life. For every one hundred men's names in the Old Testament, there are only five women's names. Many ethnic and religious traditions identify, along with the name of the deceased, only the name of a father on gravestones.

When one reads encyclopedias that provide brief biographies of historical figures, all too often the father of the famous person—his trade, personal name, and place of origin—is mentioned, but the famous person's mother won't be mentioned, even by name.

Another typical way women are lost is through the patronymical imperative which makes women change their names. Una Stannard points out that today the average woman has three different identities during her lifetime: her original one and that of two husbands. Furthermore, with every husband, the woman feels obliged to change her name on her social security card, her driver's license, her passport, bank accounts, credit cards, and voter registration, and other membership cards and legal or official documents. When women change their names, they aren't easily located anymore. Have you ever tried to trace a female friend from your high school days? You know the town she lives in, but you don't know her current married name. Unless you can find out the name of the man she married, you're helpless. Lots of women vanish this way!

It has been said that women have been written out of history. This is usually taken to mean that women's deeds, achievements, and contributions have been ignored by historians. While this is partially the case, it misses the other essential truth. Women are written out of history (personal, familial, cultural, national, and world history) because women do not have reliably consistent names as clear markers of identity. Instead women have markers of reference to relationships. Since women are nominally denied the human characteristic of durable identity and their names don't represent their unique selves as much as their relationships, and history is the writing and recollection of unique selves and their deeds, women aren't easy to place in history. A more inclusive, and therefore more authentic account of history, especially the history of families, would take into account both a male line and a female line. The writing of history so often overemphasizes lines that we forget that lines are simply conceptual schemes that facilitate but also limit understanding. An inclusive approach to history and to personal memory would be aided by the awareness that there is no equivalence between history and the story of the male line, even though they have been hitherto presented as congruent phenomena. Tracing the ancestry of women continues to be a major challenge.

Dale Spender describes the efforts of Jill Liddington and Jill Norris in their research on women's suffrage.

...Jill Liddington and Jill Norris...undertook to document the story of women's suffrage in Lancashire for this vital contribution had been largely neglected by historians. They had difficulty with sources, and one difficulty was not one which would be encountered in tracing men. "Sometimes we seemed to be forever chasing down blind alleys. For instance, one of the most active women, Helen Silcock, a weavers' union leader from Wiugan, seemed to disappear after 1902. We couldn't think why, until we came across a notice of 'congratulations to Miss Silcock on her marriage to Mr Fairhurst' in a little known labour journal, the *Women's Trade Union Review*...it was an object lesson for us in the difficulties of tracing women activists."[5]

There are unrecognized consequences for children who receive only their father's names. Children's awareness of and claim to the richness of their mother's heritage is muted by patronymy. Children live in exile from the part of themselves that could express the talents, ethnicity, and style of their female forebears.

Many people are protective of their "family name." Arthur Kurzweil, the family history expert boldly declared: "I would never change my surname!" He furthermore shakes his head incredulously over the idea that anyone could. He says, "Surnames are equally important [as first names]. I could never understand how a person could change his last name...For me, changing one's name is like cutting off an arm. It is part of you. How can you bear to lose it?"[6] But he doesn't question how women, who routinely change their names, must feel. His attitude reflects the insensitivity of our culture to what it means for women to lose their names. It doesn't even cross people's minds that it might be significant.

Another serious problem arises from the common expectation that women will someday probably change their names. Though we're not being held at gunpoint to do so, the force of custom is very strong. A man gains a progressively stronger notion of who he is, while a woman—usually at a crucial time in her identity formation, when she is a young adult—can anticipate a shift. How can women have the confidence that men have when something as essential as their name is unstable?

For anyone who lives in anticipation of a major identity rupture, a perfect adaptation strategy is to become pliant, flexible. The downside of this kind of flexibility is that you can become so potentially protean that it's hard to pinpoint the part of you that abides, the part of you that defines you. Women constantly shift the locus of their identity to transitory reference points: roles and relationships. Women lose out on the possibility of defining their personality through their actions and the public record of those actions.

Even if a woman bears the name of her husband for fifty years and has, to her own mind, psychologically appropriated it, the name is still contingent, derived. It's her husband's name on loan to her, potentially subject to symbolic foreclosure if she and he were to divorce. While she could continue to use this last name, the name would be eviscerated. It's not a name of her own, it's merely an incidental label with a semi-misrepresentative quality, since her family link with her husband has been severed. When a male is addressed by his name, he implicitly receives a chorus of affirmations. His "who-ness," his uniqueness is affirmed; his claim to his name is affirmed; his worth is affirmed. Not so for women, because women don't own their names as men do; we aren't entitled to enjoy the rights and privileges of ownership. Women are name renters. Men own names; women use them.

Now some might say that who you are changes. It's true that people's attitudes, occupations, home address, looks, and so forth change, and there are many religions that make a persuasive case for the absence of a truly enduring personal "self." Still, whether it's the truth or illusion, tacit human consensus expects us to regard ourselves and others as possessing a durable core self. Women start out with the natural experience of a durable self, but over time adopt a provisional construction of the self, which will be forever at odds with the authentically human experience of self, which is not provisional at all, but absolute, unconditional. Women's natural feelings of enduring me-ness, have to be denied if women are to socialize themselves. And so, women are forced to censor that basic experience of themselves as consistent, solid people.

The really nasty thing about all of this is that most of us who obey the contract, who eventually adapt to a construction of ourselves as referential, are shamed and punished for this. Women's construction of the self involves a process of objectification; it requires that we see ourselves and judge ourselves as others would. We are told that we don't have enough self-assuredness, confidence, take-chargeness, whatever, to be given responsibility or authority. But how is a person supposed to demonstrate a self-assured demeanor when she is nominally and socially denied the human "me" that men get to keep for life? Women are taught that in order to survive, moreover to prosper and develop as normal human beings, they must lie about their most basic existential experience, the experience that they are a discrete self. And from that first primal lie emanates the other lies and distortions that call into question women's very humanity.

One of the saddest absurdities resulting from patronymy's insistence that children bear their father's names is the symbolic exclusion of a mother from her family when she doesn't take her husband's name. Anna Quindlen wrote in *The New York Times*:

> I am on the telephone to the emergency room of the local hospital. My elder son is getting stitches in his palm, and I have called to make myself feel better, because I am at home, waiting, and my husband is there holding him. I am 34 years old, and I am crying like a child, making a slippery mess of my face. "Mrs. Krovatin?" says the nurse, and for the first time in my life I answer "Yes."
>
> This is a story about a name. The name is mine. I was given it at birth, and I have never changed it, although I married...I made my choice. I haven't changed my mind...I would never give [my name] up. Except for that one morning when I talked to the nurse at the hospital, I always answer the question "Mrs. Krovatin?" with "No, this is Mr. Krovatin's wife."[7]

Women who keep their names, but give their children their husband's last name are cast into the odd position of being symbolically in exile from the rest of their family. Their own name works in their disfavor as a kind of figurative neon sign on their chest that shrieks: "I am a feminist" or "I am holding out for a principle." Usually, women who keep their own names just want to be recognized as their own person. Yet they are punished by being relegated to the status of outsider in relation to the rest of their family, because they are the one with the oddball name.

This maternal exile is a dramatic symbolic distortion of the facts of family life. In general, the true position of mothers in our culture is at the center of the family. She performs the principal parenting tasks; she typically figures much more prominently in children's lives than their fathers do. (Nobody's saying this ought to be so, but it is.) The truth about family life is that the woman is the central figure and the man is the more remote parent. So in fact, the mother is at the center; yet nominally, she is cast to the periphery. In order to obey the terms of patronymy's contract, people have to agree to this fundamental symbolic reversal of the facts of female significance.

Patronymy can hardly be natural when it requires that more than one half of the population go through acrobatic contortions of identity. Patronymy's rules weren't here before human beings showed up and discovered them. They were invented in reference to men. Since one of the rules built into patronymy is that the rules themselves are always to be observed, patronymy reproduces itself over and over, each instance of its expression further validating and perpetuating the originally arbitrary rule. Patronymy forbids females an expansive, varied, and positive and fixed identity. It closes off the possibility of knowing ourselves as empowered, multifarious selves.

Patronymy is just one oppression that bars females from experiencing themselves as self-determining agents. It prefigures the way we interpret the value of individual women we meet or know, as well as that of the whole category of females. When males are called by name, they are affirmed; when females are called by name, they are negated.

It's no secret that we live in a culture that outwardly and secretly prefers males to females, and this fact is given strength and credence every time a woman walks around as a repository of a man's name. Until the deeply embedded notion that men take precedence over women is rooted out at the level of language, at the level of our names, we will continue to live in an environment where men are privileged over women.

Patronymy is not the cause of patriarchy, but it does keep patriarchy alive and well. Like random male violence, it is one of the vital links in the partriarchal chain that holds women back from the full freedom to be their authentic selves. In many ways, patronymy is more insidious than some of the other grosser examples of patriarchy, which can be easily identified and decried. Since patronymy, if it is recognized at all, is typically seen as a trivial custom, something akin to our culture's preferences for certain kinds of foods over others, no one does anything to change it.

The issue of what we call ourselves and our children needs to take its place alongside other fundamental feminist questions. You can't get more fundamental than names. As long as female's names represent us as being derivative of men, then the idea of women's identities being derivative of men's will be a functional part of society's collective psyche, and men will be perceived as being superior to women.

Why Patronymy Persists

Why do we put up with patronymy? Why does it persist when it is so damaging to female identity, corrosive of female self-esteem, and misrepresentative of the true nature of families? Why, against a backdrop of hard-won social reforms that benefit women, does patronymy hold sway, subverting any real possibility for lasting social respect for women? Why do we ignore this archaic practice, pretend it isn't important, and unquestioningly live by its contract? Why do so many otherwise creative people accept patronymy as necessary?

One reason patronymy persists is that, as yet, the very topic of last names has not been given due attention. Also, the last name problem doesn't readily admit one simple, obvious solution that would appeal to every individual or family.

A further obstacle is women's deep ambivalence about the potential social changes that would accompany a change in how we name ourselves. Women are well conditioned to seek evidence of their worth outside of themselves, particularly in the approving or disapproving eyes of men. Because of the crippling effects of female socialization, along with daily reinforcement by the depictions of women in the media, many women internalize a composite male standard of femaleness, a notion of female as derivative or subordinate to males. If women were to consider the topic of last names, they would be tempted to change from our male dominant naming patterns. But even to contemplate the name issue is to imperil our very cognitive foundations, our understanding of who we are and what our place is among the social strata. Many women have fortunately gotten beyond living their lives in fear of the withdrawal of male approval, but few women have been able to shed the related habit of referencing themselves to males via last names.

The fear of losing male approval is not based on foolishness. As long as there is a wage gap between men and women, and as long as social services for mothers remain scarce, most women will be financially or otherwise dependent on men at some time in their lives. Whether women are willing to admit it to themselves or not, one of the fundamental reasons why wives take husband's names and furthermore pass those names on to their children is a *quid pro quo*. Every woman knows, even if she has managed to be financially successful, that women as a class are financially disadvantaged in comparison to men. Women give in on the name issue to men so that if the going ever gets rough, or if they have to leave the work force to care for children, those men will feel some kind of responsibility to them, personal and financial since they share the same last name.

Predictably, would-be defenders of patronymy, whom we can call the preservationists, are afraid to discuss the subject because it threatens their world view based on male superiority and male entitlement. What's more surprising is that generally open-minded people are no less reluctant than the preservationists to discuss our last name customs. The subject of last names is so emotionally volatile that most people would rather distance themselves by not thinking of it as a social issue (one that affects their life and about which they need to take a stand). Instead, any deviations from last name norms, such as a woman keeping her last name at marriage or children being given their mother's last name, are understood in mainstream society as motivated by the personal taste of a few eccentrics. So the import of the subject can be easily dismissed by rationalizing that "Mary kept her last name when she married, because she was worried about losing her identity. But I don't worry about that."

The cliche is that names don't matter. But if you bother to ask, you'll find that people have surprisingly decided views about names, not only preferences for some particular names over others, but also strong views and feelings about how people ought or ought not to be named. A friend of mine who recently had her first baby reported that her mother beamed with relief when she found out that the baby wasn't given a hyphenated name. Though it doesn't make the evening news, people care more about last names than they are willing to say.

This is further corroborated by the provocative manner in which the media report naming anomalies. We get insights into the strength of the taboo against violating our last name customs when we hear accounts of famous parents who don't follow the last name rules. Magazines and newspapers gave an undue amount of space to the reports of Mia Farrow and Woody Allen's baby being given Farrow's last name, for instance.

The biggest taboo, as one might guess, involves the last names we give to children. Ethnic customs, family expectations, the practice of commemorating ancestors through names all cloud rational discussion. Male anxiety over paternity, which relates to questions of virility, along with women's efforts to reassure men, obstruct the search for satisfying solutions to the last name dilemma. Also, the historically based specter of a child's possible illegitimacy stops parents from seeking other ways of naming kids.

Whether or not a child's mother keeps her maiden name,

parents tend to give their children their father's last name even when the parents are not married. The trend among progressive couples is that the woman keeps her maiden name when the couple marries and the children take their father's name as a last name and the mother's last name as a middle name. Some couples give their child a hyphenated name, even though this proves impractical because hyphenated names can't be sustained across generations—what happens when Penelope Parnassus-Kluzewski marries Archibald Profumo-Desrosiers? Some women who raise a child without its father give the children their last names. But, it is not at all uncommon for a woman who has been deserted by the man who got her pregnant to give her child the absent father's last name.

Among progressive couples, the question of what to name the kids is a surprisingly sensitive one. When I informally asked several new parents why they chose to give their child the father's last name and the mother's name as a middle name, the best I could extract was guilt-ridden equivocations from the men and self-justifying, resigned mumbling from the women. These couples, in principle, seemed to want to be egalitarian in their choice of a last name for their children. Wives and husbands confessed uneasiness with our current naming system, but they didn't want to give their child a name that would make her or him conspicuous by being different from the norm. They worried about what would happen when the child went to school or how their parents might be upset.

The husbands awkwardly downplayed the importance of their names having won out as the names that will be officially used and perceived as the more important. The women were ambivalent; they felt as though they'd sold out. The wives also tried to downplay the significance of their decision. Several insisted that their naming decisions had been reached quite accidentally. Successful, ambitious women all, it was painful for them to face their ready acquiescence to this pervasive legacy of male supremacy. So they tended to shroud the issue in silence and pretend it was insignificant.

It is not insignificant at all. With patronymy, the father stands for the family by having all of the family's members bear his last name. While the man's name is supposedly used just to *stand for* the whole of the family, what happens conceptually and practically is that the man, by virtue of the role of his name, is assigned the predominant position within the family. There are many parts that could stand for the wholes of which they are members. Which part we pick out determines which aspect of the whole we focus on. We could have had the mother stand for the family, a reversal of patronymy, matronymy, for example. What happens is that the father's name, while it was meant to *refer* to the family, also becomes the mechanism by which we *comprehend* the family. When a part stands for the whole, other aspects of the concept are necessarily hidden as we focus on one arbitrary aspect of a concept. With patronymy, women and children are hidden as they are behind the mantle of the husband/father's patronym.

It doesn't take much imagination to come up with ideas for different ways of naming. We could toss out hereditary naming schemes altogether so that each generation could name itself, or we could give ourselves the names of trees as last names. We could just make up nonsense words that have appealing sounds, as they now do for new company's names or names of new car models. We could use the names of our occupations as last names. Many of the last names we use today are actually names of occupations or derivations therefrom, such as Taylor, Bookbinder, or Smith. Present-day versions of these occupationally based last names might include Amy Programmer, Susan Engineer, or Michael Truckdriver. Or we might create last names from personal traits or activities, for example, Dennis Runner, Kathy Singer, Myra Gardener. These suggestions strike us as fanciful, and therefore unacceptable. But *why*? They are certainly not as psychologically and socially hazardous as patronymy. Most of us reject these ideas as implausible naming strategies because they seem playful and arbitrary. We're expected to be solemn in our consideration of names and naming. And, I think, this solemnity is not inappropriate. It reflects the mostly unconscious belief that our names have a very powerful effect on how we understand and regard ourselves and what kind of impression we make on other people. Yet, I wonder whether this solemnity intimidates us to the point that we don't dare experiment with a more just way of naming. What's more than a little suspicious is that people tend to dismiss the above-mentioned alternative ways of naming as *arbitrary*. However, patronymy is just about as arbitrary a naming strategy as one could come up with. Surely with a little imagination we could come up with a naming system that would not promote a lopsided view of humanity with males as the stars in the stage production called life and females as the extras.

Indeed, there are clever and independent individuals who are experimenting with alternatives to patronymy. But their innovations are done in private, in isolation from society at large. Women haven't yet gotten together to act in concert about the issue of how we are named.

While patronymy all but edits out the fact of femaleness from consciousness and history, it does do a pretty faithful job of authentically representing how most people still *believe and wish* humanity to be ordered. This illuminates why patronymy so unrelentingly persists as our standard naming system. Patronymy is consistent with our culture's fundamental, though gradually changing, beliefs about the sexes. It simply reflects the wider reality of male dominance. Patronymy fits in perfectly with the way many believe or wish the family to be constructed and with entrenched beliefs about the comparative natural gifts of males and females.

As I write this, among other outdated laws, there is one in the state of Oklahoma that says that a husband is the official head of household and a wife must therefore by law relocate with her husband if he wants to move the family. They very term "head of household" indicates the hierarchical way in which many still think of family structure. Patronymy innocently embraces this prevalent belief or wish that the family is hierarchically structured, with husband as *ex officio* top banana. So, one of the principal reasons why most of us inexorably and unquestioningly "commit patronymy" is that in so doing, we're simply telling the truth through our naming ways about what we believe and wish.

It's embarrassing to admit, but most of us to one degree or another like patronymy. It serves us. It's useful. And, we *need* it. Or, perhaps more optimistically, it's better to say we used to need it. We needed patronymy to help us make sense of the world, to classify and order it, and to have it reflect back to us what we believe to be true about ourselves. Like any other classification scheme, patronymy has rules. Dale Spender, talking about the rules that apply to language in general, says the following, which can aptly be applied specifically to names:

> As we use these rules [for language] we confirm their validity, we make them "come true." Our results depend on the programme we begin with; as we pattern, select and interpret on the premise that

males are superior—and of course, concomitantly, that females are inferior—we construct a view of the world in which males continue to be seen as superior, and females continue to be seen as inferior, thereby perpetuating the myth and reinforcing the justification for male power...When we begin to select, pattern and interpret according to the rule that the sexes are equal, we will construct a very different reality, we will make very different ideas "come true." The claim for male superiority will no longer seem reasonable and the male monopoly in power will be seen as problematic.[1]

Patronymy is a systematically closed and self-perpetuating classification scheme that makes male dominance and male superiority "come true." If we wish to make different ideas come true, we either have to abandon naming systems altogether (which would be unlikely to happen) or create a new system which makes better ideas (such as the equality of the sexes) come true.

The cultural habit of patronymy contributes to its convenience as a naming option, because individuals and families don't have "to trouble themselves" with coming up with a new way to name themselves and classify kinship relationships. All people have to do is plug into patronymy. No muss, no fuss, no naming problem.

Patronymy persists because "This is the way we've always done it, so it must be right!" Large groups of people do things that are not necessarily virtuous or admirable, smoking cigarettes, for instance. The rightness or justice of a practice has nothing to do with how long it's been done or whether it has mass support. Received wisdom has not always proved itself to be wise.

But, patronymy's persistence goes much deeper than social habit. Though patronymy primarily advances male interests, women, too, invoke patronymy to gain advantage as, for example, when a woman brags about marrying into a family with a prestigious name, then commandeers that name for purposes of self-aggrandizement. But patronymy's categories and images for the most part rationalize and justify in myriad subtle and not so subtle ways the existing social order—patriarchy—as natural, necessary, and just. Patronymy is a kind of lubricant to the commonplace inequities between the sexes that occur in everyday social interactions: the routine coercions, discrediting, and domination, the dispensation of privileges and authority, and the ordinary manipulations that occur in the work place, the family, and in all manner of public settings.

Patronymy's defenders insist that it must be the best naming system because so many people follow the custom without coercion. But is there really no coercion? Women are socially harassed in an overt or subtle spoken or unspoken way if they don't conform to the custom of taking their husband's names. A wife is made to feel selfish if she wants to keep her own name or pass her name on to her kids. People will call into question the quality of her love: "If you really loved him, you would take his name." Women are similarly shamed into passing the patronym to their children by the argument that it's in the best interests of the children.

Two can't become one. The insistent sentimentalization of marriage as a union by popular and high culture only serves to rationalize and recreate patronymy. But marriage is not union, and two do not become one flesh. It is two discrete individuals going together on a mutual life journey. Women are bulldozed into changing their names and giving their kids their husband's names by the cultural propaganda that misrepresents the nature of marriage as union. Since in reality two can't really become one, something has to give, *someone* has to give, and that someone is the woman. Males can wax rhapsodic about this union business because they don't give anything up. When women marry, they give up an elemental part of their identity in service of building up their husband's.

Women expect that they will give up their names when they marry—this is part and parcel of the romance of union. A fundamental liability of marriage gets transformed into an ambition, something to look forward to. Many wedding ceremonies still close with the priest or minister declaring, "I now present Mr. and Mrs. John Doe."

WHY WE LIKE PATRONYMY

Patronymy persists because it contains some of our most cherished values. For instance, it confers an apparent sense of family unity on a group of people who share the same surname. When I interviewed people about their name choices, many otherwise free-thinking couples said that the wife took her husband's last name and the children were given the father's last name because they "wanted to be one family." What is overlooked in this thinking is that this wished for familial unity is, through names, only symbolic. It's not a truthful or comprehensive representation of one family since it was created through the amputation of a married woman's name and all the senses and personalities it comprises. Patronomy creates a partial representation passed off as a complete one. Patronymical last names can't successfully evoke both the unity of the family and the multiplicity of its constituents. It's not that families can't functionally be units. Some are; some aren't. Having all members of a primary family share the same patronymical last name is no insurance that a family will be unified in spirit. There are plenty of families whose members share a patronymical last name, but through divorce the family is fractured.

Another payoff of patronymy is that it simplifies for bureaucracies and individuals the challenge of keeping track of kin relations. Patronymy does a fair job of helping people express their connections to their antecedents. Although it does provide nominal generational links to our ancestors, these links are only partial since matronymical information is disregarded.

Patronymy creates a semblance of social and bureaucratic expediency. It appears to have a simplicity which makes it seem attractive and reasonable. Yet, we have to remember that expedience always exacts a price. Patronymy's apparent efficiency in identifying people and locating them within a set of kinship relations is questionable. While patronymy consolidates family ties, it does so by tossing out all the female information that lives within female names (which includes information about male antecedents, of course). This attachment to patronymy's supposed expediency has resulted in a collective failure of the imagination. It has blinded us to the possibility of other expeditious, simple, and more egalitarian solutions to the problem of last names.

If we want to rethink the last name dilemma and come up with a new, more appropriate naming strategy that reflects the true extent to which women direct the course of public and private life; if we are to "begin to select, pattern and interpret according to the rule that the sexes are equal" so that "we will make very different ideas come true," we cannot afford to be insensitive to the needs that patronymy currently fulfills.

People who follow the rules of patronymy's contract are not necessarily weak-willed or uncritical. There are plenty of women who make name choices for themselves and their children that are consistent with patronymy, who did so for their own reasons. Some women adopt the traditional naming course because they recognize its social and bureaucratic expedience. Certainly the traditional choice often forestalls censure from one's community. Some may have grown up with a name that provoked jeering in the school yard and welcomed the opportunity to change their maiden name— what an odious term—to one that is more euphonious or less obtrusive. Still others, who weren't crazy about their fathers or their families, are relieved to renounce their maiden names and thereby mark a new stage of life and commitment with the adoption of a new name.

HOW PATRONYMY BOLSTERS MEN'S CONFIDENCE

To really understand why patronymy is not challenged and why then it seems as though it will always be with us, we have to focus on how children are named. The custom of children taking their father's names could be said to have been established when women started taking their husband's last names as a matter of course. The tradition of patronymics in Europe, and especially in England, intersected with women taking their husband's names at marriage, which consolidated these customs into patronymy as we know it.

Patronymy, which is based on common law principles, provides that a legitimate child bears the name of its father. Historically, so-called illegitimate children were given their mothers' surnames at birth.[2] The mothers of such children suffer social ostracism, while the fathers of illegitimate children bear no such stigma. These biological fathers of illegitimate children may be viewed as irresponsible, but they are more often forgotten, and they certainly aren't stigmatized in the conventional way that unmarried women are. There is no paternal counterpart to society's sneering epithet, "unwed mother." This is because the real definition of a bastard is a child that a woman dared, or by necessity had to, bring into the world herself. In just about every Western language there is at least one vicious epithet denoting a person who was born "illegitimately." The growing incidence of single mothers by choice should erode the mean-spirited sense of the expression.

The concept of illegitimacy was made up and continues to be a meaningful concept to our society because it devalues women's central role with respect to the creation of life and elevates the males'.

I believe males feel existentially illegitimate, and they project their collective uneasiness and shame about this onto women and children. None of us know why we're alive or why there is life at all, but males feel the question, "Why am I here, for what purpose was I created" acutely. Males look around and observe that there really is no obviously necessary thing for them to do. Life itself does not assign them any obvious or *ipso facto* vocation. Males look at women and see that they can grow life within them and sustain that life with breast milk after they give birth.

I'm not saying that women don't have their share of existential reflective moments. All I'm saying is that females have the potential to do something significant that directly affects the fact of human existence. Males have to make up their purpose. While men's role in creation is essential but small, women's role is essential and big. At a very basic level, males can be said to be minor characters in the drama of the human species.

The hard facts are that once the sperm has been contributed, women physically create and nurture life; that is, they can create families without a whit of help from men. More to the point, if it can be said that there is something such as a family, women and children are its natural constituents. Men, on the other hand, are provisional members. Theoretically, it is through women's consent that men get to be part of families at all. Women can and do bring into being and maintain families without men. Once a woman has a fertilized egg, she has the beginning of a family.

Men feel illegitimate with respect to creating life, the most exalted work in the universe. This feeling is accompanied by a nagging sense that with respect to family life, they might be in a fundamental sense irrelevant. They feel left out and don't know for what purpose they were created.

So, what do males do? They shame women for having the gift of giving life, and they devalue women's role as principal parent so that they don't have to recognize that males are biologically extraneous to the family after mating has taken place. It's not that males are socially irrelevant to families, it's that their relevance is human-made; it's not fundamental in any biological sense. The notion of illegitimacy is a convention by which a woman and her child are to be despised unless they acknowledge the role, the fact of the father. And this is done by conferring the father's name on the child.

Women and children are the formal constituents of families, but patronymy would have us believe that families are composed of men and their children with an incidental mother. While the whole patronymy/legitimacy issue evolved to clarify inheritance and to keep the control of wealth in male hands, patronymy also continues to function as a sop women throw to men to shield them from their uneasy peripheral status within families. "Okay, Buster, you can put your name on our children, but you better support the family and pitch in. You better do something relevant and helpful here." This is the basic nominal trade-off between men and women.

Since the man's last name persists (while female names die out) and functions as the all-embracing designation for the family, the father's position in the family is given an importance that is well out of proportion to his actual place and demotes the mother's role. Under patronymy, women marry into a man's family and the male is the nominal head of the family. What a blatant and arrogant misrepresentation of the facts. Women are the "heads of families."

Patronymy is the palpable evidence of men's morbid fear of existential irrelevance. Women can do everything that men can do *and* they can give birth. The grand nominal reversal that has been perpetrated is that children automatically get their father's last names (to protect them from the mark of illegitimacy), not because men are thought to be the more important parent, but because they are known to be the *less* important parent, the remote parent. The automatic practice of conferring the patronym on a child as a stamp of legitimacy is nothing more than a vain attempt by men and women to symbolically redress the imbalance of comparative capability between women and men. The principal reason that patronymy persists, even when it fails to preserve the identities of over half the population and renders children's names dependent on their mother's marital status is that it preserves a myth that is very important to the stability of society. The myth is that men are fundamentally vital to the family.

A Brief History of Patronymy

Many arguments for patronymy reduce to "If there were a better way to name ourselves, instead of following the patronymical pattern, someone would have thought of it before and put their new system into practice." Just because our parents didn't come up with something different from patronymy doesn't mean that we shouldn't. These false arguments, which are just disguised resistance to social change, are based on misapprehension. Patronymy, in the form we know it, has not actually been around that long, nor has it been universally practiced in the Western world.

Surnames of any kind were not used in Europe until about the eleventh century, and they didn't become common until the end of the sixteenth century. Some women started taking their husbands' names when they married around the thirteenth century; among aristocratic families, women did so for prestige.

As commerce in cities developed, there arose an increasing need to distinguish among, say, all the men named John, in order to establish who owned a piece of property, or whatever. So-called family names evolved from individual surnames. These surnames, which used to vary among related individuals or even within the life of a person as she or he changed occupations, for example, eventually became hereditary.

Many insular or isolated rural communities were not

affected as readily by these proto-patronymical events. These communities just used given names or given names along with unfixed surnames, such as place names, patronymics (which are names derived from one's father's name, usually rendered in a form meaning "son of *father's name*" for a boy and "daughter of *father's name*" for a girl), descriptive names, occupational names, and matronymics ("Sara, daughter of Rebecca").

For example, while for centuries the communities around them were using patronymical last names, the Jews in the ghettos of Central and Eastern Europe used only given names and patronymics. It wasn't until the late eighteenth and early part of the nineteenth century that Jews had to choose or were given family names. In Austria, the first year that Jews were required to register last names was 1787. Jews in Switzerland didn't have to register last names until 1863. Even when they did begin using last names, European Jews did not universally adopt the last name of their fathers. Very frequently children would be given their mother's birth name rather than their father's. Among the persecutions that Jews suffered in Europe, they were often restricted from having their marriages recognized by civil law, so that when Jewish children were born, they would be considered illegitimates. Civil law would compel the parents to give these so-called illegitimate children their mother's last name. Even as recently as just before World War II in Eastern Europe, there were several Jewish communities which more often than not conferred the mothers' last name on the children rather than the fathers'.

Swedes did not use last names as we know them until the beginning of the nineteenth century. Before that they used patronymics. H. L. Mencken, in reporting the observations of E. Gustav Johnson, describes Swedish naming practices thus:

...the son of Johann Gustafsson, on being baptized with his grand-father's given name, became Gustaf Johansson, and his son in turn, was Johann after his grandfather, and became Johann Gustafsson... some Christian names would be continued in a family from genera-tion to generation, but no definite family name would be associated with them. When these patronymics began to be made permanent a difficulty arose, for a daughter who, in the past, would have been Anna Gustafsdotter, became Anna Gustafsson, which set the yokels to tittering. In time people got used to it.[1]

Norwegians also used patronymics while other European communities had converted over to the last name systems that resemble our present-day one. When Norwegians arrived in great numbers in the United States in the mid-nineteenth century, they had to convert their patronymics and the names of their homeland family farms, which had also been used as surnames, into patronymical last names. Patronymics are still in use in Iceland and in the Shetland Islands.

Patronymics seem to be an evolutionary predecessor to patronymical last names. While they still make central the paternal relationship to children over the maternal one, they were more like labels than names as we know them today.

Una Stannard believes that the practice of giving children their father's surnames sprang from people's ignorance of the facts of life. It was thought that males contributed the seed of life, while the female womb provided the soil in which the seed grew. It wasn't until 1827 that the female ovum was discovered, and even then it was thought to be merely a source of nutrition.[2] Since the female role in generation was thought to be neglible, it seemed only logical that children would receive their names from their fathers, who were seen as the sole progenitors.

Different Ways of Naming Ourselves

Historical and cross-cultural examples of other naming systems abound. Some of them have attractive features, while others have features that are even more noisome than patronymy's. These examples provide concrete evidence that it's quite possible for people to live with last name systems very different from our current one. We can also see the historically and culturally accidental nature of patronymy.

A surprisingly broad-minded naming practice was prevalent in medieval France. Female children were given their mother's birth name and male children were given their father's birth name.

Many contemporary communities in Iceland and the Soviet Union use patronymics in combination with a patrilineally inherited family name. Russians insert the patronymic between the first name and the family name. If a father's name is Ivan Sokolov, then the son's name, for example, would be Viktor (first name) Ivanovich (patronymic) Sokolov (family), and the daughter's name would be, for example, Katya (first name) Ivanovna (patronymic meaning daughter of Ivan) Sokolova (family name with feminine ending). A person is typically addressed by their first name and their patronymic.

In Czechoslovakia fairly recent legislation provides that both a husband and a wife can retain their birth names or the wife may take her husband's patronymical family name, or the husband may take his wife's patronymical family name.

The present-day naming systems of Spain, Portugal, and other Latin countries are more equitable than our English-based system, and they prove that primary families (one generation consisting of parents and children) can be perfectly stable without the glue of everyone bearing the same patronymical last name. Spanish families are no less intact than ours (and we don't have much to brag about anyway given the current rate of divorce in North America) and *husbands and wives have different last names.*

Here's how the Spanish system works: When children are born — males or females—they are given a legal name which they will officially use for life. That name consists of a first name and *two* fully functional surnames which are not hyphenated. Almost universally the first surname comes from the father and the second surname comes from the mother. The name from one's mother is in the same position as our "last name" under the English-based system. However, the Spanish system is still patrilineal. It is generally the first surname (which looks like a middle name to us) that carries more social weight. Even though the surname of the father descends to future generations and the surname of the mother doesn't, at one generational level a person bears, and never loses or changes, both their father's and mother's (patrilineal) surname.

For instance, if a woman named Ada Garcia Lopez were to marry a man named Juan Solis Padua, they would each keep their respective full names for life. If this couple had children, their kids—be they male or female—would be named Baby #1 Solis Garcia, Baby #2 Solis Garcia, and so on.

Spain recently passed a law which permits couples to name their children by placing the mother's surname or the father's surname in either the first or the second position.

The sequence of the names is entirely up to the parents. In practice, most parents are still following tradition, placing the father's surname first and the mother's second. But, there are couples who are reversing the traditional order for aesthetic and social reasons. Still, with almost no exception, it is the female's father's name that travels lineally, regardless of the order in which the surnames are arranged.

Under some circumstances, such as on a married woman's passport, her legal name will be listed along with the phrase "de *her husband's name*," as in Isabella Mendes Cardozo de Lopez. This is not her legal name. Her legal name, as we said before, is the one given to her at birth. The "de Lopez" is an identifying description used to establish her marital relationship, but it's not what she's called on a day-to-day basis.

In aristocratic circles, a woman will sometimes be referred to by her first name plus the construction "*de her husband's name*." This is done when a woman has married a particularly well-known or rich man. Both the surnames of her father and mother are dropped, but once again, this is not the norm, nor is it her "real" name. And, even if she is often referred to as Ada de Solis, one of her original surnames is always known to her community because her children bear it.

The contemporary Spanish naming system, though still patrilineal, is an enormous improvement on our English system because of the following points:

- Everyone has the same name for life, whether or not they marry.

- Husbands and wives legally and (generally) socially have their own surnames; neither spouse has to give up a name.

49

- Children bear a surname that their father bore as well as a surname from their mother.

- One of the mother's names, even though it is derived patrilineally, is not forgotten because her children bear it for life.

- In spite of the fact that the mother's name is patrilineally derived, it does refer to her identity and thereby implies an explicit valuing of female and maternal heritage.

Still, the Spanish system is less than ideal in that female names are not accorded the status of generational travel.

Free spirits have been ignoring the prevailing naming customs for a long time. In 1855 the abolitionist, acclaimed public speaker, and women's rights leader, Lucy Stone, insisted on keeping her own name after she married Henry Brown Blackwell. Journalist Ruth Hale, her successor in name pioneering, established the Lucy Stone League in New York in 1921 to establish and protect the right of married women to keep their own names. Hale kept her own name when she married Heywood Broun in 1917. The story goes that when Hale was coming back down the aisle after her wedding, some well-meaning person made a blunder by calling out "Hello, Mrs. Heywood Broun," and Hale supposedly barked back, "I am not Mrs. Heywood Broun. I am Ruth Hale. Don't ever call me Mrs. Broun." When people phoned her at home, asking for Mrs. Broun, she would brusquely say, "Mrs. Broun does not live here," and would give them the phone number of her husband's mother. If she ever received an invitation to a party or an event addressed to Mr. and Mrs. Broun, she wouldn't respond to it. The only member of her household whom she would acknowledge as "Mrs. Heywood Broun" was her cat. Ruth Hale's and Heywood Broun's son, the famous sportswriter, was named Heywood Hale Broun.

In Canada, according to civil law, everyone can use any name they like, as long as they are not trying to defraud anyone. There is no law that requires a bride to take her husband's surname. In fact, in the province of Quebec, the law requires that women retain their maiden names for official purposes throughout life. Before the 1970s, most Canadian women changed their surnames at marriage, but many now opt to retain their birth names. In Britain there is also a practice of combining the patronymical family names of the married couple into a hyphenated form.

Amish communities in southeastern Pennsylvania frequently give their children the mother's maiden name as a middle name. Amish children's names thereby represent two family lines, because middle names are accorded more attention than they are in mainstream America. More girls are given their mother's maiden surname for a middle name than boys.

NEW WAYS OF NAMING IN THE U.S.

Today, most of the people in the U.S. who are naming themselves and their children counter to convention follow certain trends that were established by name pioneers of the '60s and '70s.

The Hyphenators
We're all familiar with the hyphenators: those women and the very occasional men who dare to put principles ahead of euphony. While hyphenating is a step toward an egalitarian

naming procedure, its disadvantage becomes apparent as soon as a couple with a hyphenated last name contemplates grandchildren. If the hyphenators' children were to continue their parents' naming strategy, their child would be the unfortunate bearer of a name that would look something like this: Karen Clarissa Phillips-Barnette-Stuart-Aronson. How does this poor soul introduce herself? And, what happens when Karen has children!

Hyphenation isn't practical as a workable successor to patronymy as it doesn't work across generations. And let's face it, aren't those hyphenated names clunky? Also, people often forget or ignore the woman's birth name. While there are some well-meaning husbands who take the hyphenated name along with their wives, people consistently lop off the first (the woman's) surname when they address the men. It's similar to earlier innovations in language which resulted in women being referred to as "Chairperson" and men being referred to as "Chairmen."

Lucy Stoners

Just like the famous nineteenth-century social reformer and suffragist who kept her own name as a matter of principle when she married, the Lucy Stoners retain their original last name (that is, we must note, their *father's* family name).

The Double Agents

Double Agents think they can have their cake and eat it too. These women hopefully but erroneously imagine that one can actually sustain two names simultaneously: their birth names in business, their husbands' surnames socially. Because of the tendency among husbands, relatives, friends, and associates to see a woman's birth name, *even if she declares that she is keeping her own name after marriage*, as provisional and the husband's name as the *real* name, every time a woman makes the smallest capitulation, active or passive, to the convention of married women assuming their husband's name, she increasingly loses her ability to uphold what she regards as her true name. Every time she refrains from correcting someone who refers to her by her husband's name on a letter, during a social introduction, etc., she slowly erodes her claim to her rightful name.

You can't maintain two names and preserve the existential vitality of both. One (almost universally, the woman's birth name) will recede in importance and become a label or a title, or at best a pseudonym (which literally means false name), not a name. Whenever there is ambiguity, people will defer to tradition and use the husband's last name.

Reluctant Renegades

Reluctant Renegades are sensible if timid moderates. They know that hyphenated names get mutilated or lost within the unavoidable bureaucracies we have to appease to get driver's licenses, college diplomas, or tax refunds. Reluctant renegades like a smooth sail and don't want to be bothered with social awkwardness or obtuse bureaucrats to prove some point. So they choose to be inconspicuously principled by retaining their last names as their middle or penultimate names, while taking their husbands' family names as their last names.

The essential drawback of this naming choice is that the woman's maiden name usually gets hidden behind the mantle of her husband's name. The effect of retaining her maiden name ends up being for her private satisfaction only. She is still seen by others as Mrs. Husband, or even Ms. Husband.

The Customizers

When Alice Jacobs and Ken Balford got married, each

of them gave up their last name. Together they picked a brand new name, MacDonald, which they both adopted. They are now known as Alice and Ken MacDonald. The name Mac-Donald had no family associations for either one of them; they simply liked the sound of MacDonald and liked the fact that they chose the name jointly. Alice and Ken were attached to the idea of their having the same last name along with their children, but they didn't think that one of them should have to give up their last name and be swept under the mantle of the other's last name. That they came up with a brand new custom name was an assertion of their unique relationship.

This naming solution is appealing in that it promotes a sense of unity for a primary family, because all family members have the same last name. However, many people would object to this symbolic amputation of ties to antecedents.

The Amalgams

Law professor Frederica Lombard has given serious consideration to the idea of a child's name being an amalgam of each of the parents' surnames.

> A child of Mary Miller and John Brown might be Baby Millbrown or Brownmill. In some situations, this solution might prove useful, but it is clear that not all names can be artistically amalgamated. And the issue of whose name should go first is always potentially troublesome. Even for those names that can be combined, aesthetic issues of how they should be combined remain if the parties themselves cannot agree, and individual judges are not always possessed of finely tuned aesthetic senses which would enable them to reach solutions acceptable to all litigants concerned.[1]

In a more humorous vein, a woman whose last name was Solomon got involved with a man whose last name was Watson. They both philosophically opposed eclipsing one of their identities by using only one person's last name, yet they wanted to share the same last name to proclaim their relationship. Their solution was to create a hybrid of their last names. They consequently became known as the "Sowats" (pronounced "So Whats").

Another kind of amalgam was tried by a couple whose first names were Kay and Lee. Their children's last name is now Kaylee. Their strategy does satisfy the prevalent desire to provide nominal linkage between generations and it commemorates one's forebears. It can also, theoretically travel across generations because Sue Kaylee who marries Gary Wise can together have children named Bill and Jane Suegary or Garysue. Still, while this strategy is simple to implement, the potential for widespread adoption is negligible because there are lots of first names that do not mesh well with other first names to form satisfying compound last names. Imagine the fate of children born to parents whose first names are Alexandra and Herbert.

Unique Names

Since under patronymy, female last names are expected to change, women are more free to experiment with names, to try on given names and surnames. Accordingly, many women have actively used the adoption of their husbands' names as a way of turning over a new leaf or setting their lives on a new course. Others have designed unique names for themselves irrespective of marriage. Since females aren't beholden to their birth last names to the degree that males are, females can make their names *meaningful*. Religions have long been aware of the real link between name changes and deep inner changes of a psychological or spiritual nature. Many cultures have naming ceremonies whose premise is the direct relationship between a change in name and a radical transformation of the individual. Recognizing this spiritual link between names and the self, many women have named themselves uniquely.

Countless women are adopting propitious names with symbolic associations, particularly inspired by the women's spirituality movement. Many women are using their mother's maiden names as last names. Some are using the names of female luminaries of the past from whom they can draw inspiration. Some women are using the first or last name of a distant inspiring female ancestor. Some women are using new names whose sounds appeal to them or names that more obviously express their ethnic or religious identity. As women are getting in touch with their unique selves and with the people and values that have shaped them, they are creating correspondingly unique names. A few examples include Lindsey River, Una Stannard, Starhawk, Jane Fire, Patrice Wynne, Hallie Iglehart Austen, Asphodel, Chela Blitt, Alia Almeida Agha, Biaja Teal, Vicki Noble, Karen Goodwoman, Susan Elizabeth, and Shere Hite.

Matronymy

There are a few courageous cases in which the man of a couple takes his wife's surname. In choosing to flaunt convention, those few men have drawn attention to the absurdity of society's expectation that women should automatically take their husband's names. Still, this bold name choice is vulnerable to criticism for being just as arbitrary or sexist as the compulsory practice of women taking their husband's names. We have to applaud these male name pioneers for their matronymical gestures. They are helping symbolically to redress the damage done by patronymy and acknowledge the woman's actual position in the family and the high degree of influence she exerts over family life. Some people have persuasively argued that matronymy is a more expedient and commonsensical naming scheme than patronymy because people always know who the biological mother of a child is.

The chances for widespread adoption of matronymy is slight because matronymy commits the same sins as patronymy. It could also be financially and socially devastating to women and children if fathers' role in the family were not nominally instantiated.

NEW WAYS OF NAMING OUR CHILDREN

When it comes to naming children, even the free spirits described above tend to name their children according to patronymy's rules. Still, there are some brave souls who have broken out of the patronymical mold in naming their children.

The Alternators

These are the people who give one of the parents' last name to the first child, and the other parent's last name for the second child, and so forth. The spirit behind such a practice seems admirable, and obviously couples who choose this route evince a sensitivity to the problem posed by patronymy.

Alternating is a good idea in spirit as it enacts egalitarian principles if it is applied faithfully. There are intrinsic problems of course. What if a couple has only one child? Then there is the problem of precedence: Whose name gets passed on first?

Matronymics

Some parents have found the use of matronymics, names that are derived from a mother's name, useful. A classic example is "Freyda Lucychild." Once again, the informing spirit is admirable, but the particular executions of such a system are dubious. We have the same problem as we have with amalgams. Some names sound okay with -child or -daughter and some don't. Furthermore, this system excludes the male's role in generation and family life.

Matronymy

This is just like patronymy, but with the sex bias reversed. Children would, as a matter of course, receive their mother's names instead of their father's. The historical specter of symbolic illegitimacy and male objections would prevent this from ever being a real successor to patronymy.

Hyphenating Surnames

Hyphenating a child's parents' last names has the same problems it has for adult hyphenators, with the added problem that such a constructed name makes a child stand out oddly among his or her peers, which could be hard on a child. It's also not fair to burden children by having their names announce their parents' principles.

Unique Names

There is the whole question of whether or not we should bother with lineages at all. Some couples have opted for giving a child a first name, and perhaps a middle name, and a last name that comes from neither the mother nor the father. For example Jane Fonda and Tom Hayden named their son Troy O'Donovan Garity.

No Last Name

While perfectly legal, it is unlikely that most people would be willing to part with last names of some kind. Too many bureaucracies depend on the fact of last names.

People who adopt this naming approach for their children are setting their kids up for a life full of petty annoyances. It is fun to imagine what it would be like though. If adopted on a large scale, this strategy would force the pool of first names to be much larger, and parents would be more inclined to think of unique names for their children, as Native Americans and African tribes people have for centuries.

Children of Reluctant Renegades

A current naming trend is to give a child its father's last name and its mother's last name as the child's middle name. A variation is to give the child the father's last name, but the mother's first name as a first or middle name. There is goodwill behind such decisions, but the main feature of patronymy—the inevitability of the child receiving his father's last name—is retained. While this naming approach honors the mother, it does so for but one generation.

Children's Choice

Some people have said that children who have to live with their names should be the ones to chose them. This flexible approach to names has romantic, but not practical appeal. Children have to be named shortly after they are born, and immediately their identities take shape in relation to their names. By the time the child is mature enough to understand the consequences of choosing a name, the original birth name would have "gelled."

Gloria Steinem suggested that "...children would be better identified by having both parents' last names, thus saving millions of people-hours now spent explaining, 'This is my daughter by my second marriage...' At 16 or 18 children could choose their own last names, from their parents or otherwise, as part of becoming their own unique selves."[2] It could be awkward for children to have to choose between their parents. This proposal also doesn't prescribe the sequence of the parents' last names.

Those who are countering name convention are isolated from one another. All of the naming innovations we have discussed in this chapter are important because each contributes to realizing the arbitrariness of patronymy's contract. Yet, not one of them seems to be an appropriate candidate to succeed patronymy. What can we do collectively?

A Name For Life:
The Bilineal Solution

In order to replace patronymy with another naming system, a large number of women and couples have to embrace one consistent solution to the last name dilemma.

If we're going to change how we are named and all of its entailments, most of us will need to name by a new, collectively agreed-to contract. Everyone else can commit nominal anarchy, which supports the cause of overturning patronymy anyway. Real change in language as it reflects on the sexes is possible. For example, in spite of the protests of grammarians and *The New York Times*, Ms. became standard American English because many people used it in respectable settings, and it filled a real social and linguistic need.

How do we choose a naming system that will appeal to the greatest number of people and yet not compromise our goal of having an egalitarian system that preserves those parts of our current naming system that serve real needs of the human spirit?

Our new system will be just as biased as patronymy, but we should be forthcoming about our biases. The world view we wish to advance embraces the conviction that females as a category of human beings are as good in every respect as men, that women's activities, identities, *female meanings* are absolutely essential to the enrichment and preservation of human life.

CRITERIA FOR A NEW WAY OF NAMING

- It must embody present-day values.

- It must reflect the contemporary roles and true extent of women's influence.

- It should be conservative; *i.e.*, it should cohere with the current naming convention so that most people will welcome it.

- It must be easy to understand and easy to apply.

- It should be a naming system that can be passed from generation to generation.

For a new convention to really take hold, it not only has to satisfy a need that is shared by a great number of people, but it also has to appeal to people whose tastes, habits, customs, mores, and political orientations are very different from our own. And, of course, since naming is ultimately a matter of individual choice, I am not asking people to adopt it absolutely. It's not a question of promulgating a new law, but of instituting a new custom that accommodates differences in human tastes. To try to coerce all people into adopting one naming system or another is unrealistic and doctrinaire.

We should begin by asking whether we should continue having hereditary last names at all. People are attached to patronymy because it creates lineages. There is a deep human desire to symbolically represent the links among generations. In setting up a hereditary scheme, we must acknowledge that only a limited amount of ancestral information can be transmitted across generations without creating unwieldy names. Until recently, the assumption was that female ancestral information would necessarily yield to the males, which in effect made it die out. This is what we want to rectify.

A crucial guiding principle in the development of a new convention is that its rules must not be too loosely defined, flexible, or permissive. There shouldn't be allowance for idiosyncratic adaptations. Instability is built into the system if too many options are possible. When it comes to naming, people want rules, and they want clear-cut ones. There is room for creativity in deciding on first names and second names (what are usually called middle names) for children. While it appeals to our creative and anti-authoritarian impulses to discard rules or set up a naming system that allows maximum accommodation to individual tastes, such flexibility would mean that particular points of this naming scheme would be subject to negotiation. If we leave the rules up to settlement through negotiation, the naming process could become a battlefield, one where stronger personalities within a family would win out. By having the rules of this new naming scheme clearly spelled out, we guard against violation of the egalitarian principles it is intended to protect. In the absence of clear rules, an alternative naming system will break down and almost everyone will revert to the incumbent authority of patronymy.

The Bilineal Solution

What follows is a summary of the features of a simple and egalitarian naming system for ourselves and for our children. When someone says in so many words that we're stuck with patronymy, you can now say, "No we're not," and explain the Bilineal Solution!

1. Establish a *Source Name*

2. People who marry each keep their own last name

3. Girls take mother's last name

4. Boys take father's last name

5. Girls take father's last name as a middle name

6. Boys take mother's last name as a middle name

How To Practice the Bilineal Solution

Establish your source name. Your source name is the last name you wish to go by for life. Whether you are male or female, your source name has the potential to be transmitted to future generations, if you have children. To establish your source name from which future generation's names will radiate, you must shift your perspective on names from passive reception to active choice. As the first generation instituting the Bilineal Solution, we have the unique opportunity to decide whether or not we have the right name, bearing in mind aesthetic, ethnic, psychological, religious, and spiritual considerations.

Your source name may be the one you bear right now. It might be a name you took upon marriage. It could be the name you were given at birth but gave up when you got married. You can also make up your source name. You could chose a name that memorializes that ancestor of yours who figures prominently in family legend. You could choose the name of an inspirational historical figure. You can make up a name with a sound you like. You can follow naming customs of old and give yourself a source name based on your occupation, the place where you live, or a character or physical trait that distinguishes you. You can adopt the last name your grandfather had before it was shortened or anglicized when he immigrated to America. Out of respect for the power of names—the lore they generate, the personal impression they project, the ancestral identities they evoke—your choice should be made in a thoughtful way. Whether it consists of affirming your birth name or current name as "the right name" or changing your name to the right one, establishing your source name is a unique opportunity to infuse your name with meaning that will resonate across time through the future generations who will bear it.

Keep your name for the rest of your life, even if you marry. Everyone now and in future generations can go through a lifetime with a durable, uninterrupted name and correspondingly durable identity. No one has to, as a matter of custom, be subject to the petty bureaucratic annoyances, hidden expenses, and inconveniences of compulsory name changes. *Everyone* keeps their first and last names for life.

Girls are given their mother's last name and boys are given their father's last name. This creates a matrilineage in addition to a patrilineage. Female last names are preserved for generations to come just as male last names are. Males have been able to declare "I am John Jones, son of Samuel Jones, grandson of Raymond Jones and I have a son named Peter Jones and a grandson named Mark Jones." Under the Bilineal Solution, they can continue to do so. The bonus is that females can now similarly declare, "I am Susan Smith, daughter of Mary Smith, granddaughter of Barbara Smith, and I have a daughter named Carol Smith and a granddaughter named Michelle Smith."

Girls are given their father's last name as a middle name and boys are given their mother's last name as a middle name. This creates for children a nominal link with both parents and contributes to a nominal representation of family unity, since everyone has the same family names, but in a different order for boy and girl children. The structure of children's names looks like this:

Girls' Names = First name, Dad's last name, Mom's last name.

Boys' Names = First name, Mom's last name, Dad's last name.

For example, my name is Sharon Lebell. I am married to John Loudon. Our daughters' names are Misha Loudon Lebell and Kyle Dylan Loudon Lebell (in Kyle's case, we decided to also give her a second name). In general, for the public's purposes, our children are referred to as Misha Lebell and Kyle Lebell, but the fact that they both have their father's name provides a nominal link to him. If we were to have a boy, his name might be Joshua Lebell Loudon. On a day-to-day basis, he would be known as Joshua Loudon, but his formal records would reflect his longer, more inclusive name.

ADAPTING THE BILINEAL SOLUTION TO YOUR PERSONAL NEEDS

You now have the rudiments of the Bilineal Solution. All that remains is to encourage your children to keep their names for life and to pass on their names to their children in accordance with the Bilineal Solution. Whereas the basic rules of the Bilineal Solution are straightforward, this system can be quite flexible in order to suit an individual's or family's special naming needs or preferences. For instance, if a couple likes the idea of sharing their last names to symbolize their love and connection, each may take the other's last name as their middle name, superseding their given middle name. This way both wife and husband still keep their last name for life, so their public identity remains undisturbed by their marriage. Another example: if a single mother is raising a son without his biological father, she can give the baby her father's last name, thereby joining her baby boy to the male lineage of her family. If a family wishes to not only give a child a first name but a second name as well (what has formally been called a middle name), they can easily do so, and the child simply has four names.

The Advantages of the Bilineal Solution

Of all the naming solutions to the last name dilemma, the Bilineal Solution is the only one that has all of the following advantages:

- It is easy to understand, easy to use, easy to switch to, and easy to explain.

- It preserves the maximum number of worthwhile features of patronymy (thereby appealing to the human propensity for gradual and moderate social change, and it discards what is not useful, relevant, or salubrious to females.

- It respects the names and identity of all people. Male names and female names are accorded the same importance. Boys won't be favored over girls in the way that they have been until now, since it has been only males who could pass their names to their progeny.

- It preserves a nominal representation of family unity at the level of the current generation.

- It simply and elegantly maintains generational ties with ancestors and descendants.

- It affirms a person for being the sex he or she is.

- It prevents the problem of precedence, namely the question of whose family name goes first, which is found in other naming systems.

- The parameters for naming are clear: there is not a lot of opportunity for self-styled and biased interpretation, which could otherwise undermine the egalitarian spirit of the system. This obviates the need for naming decisions based on subjective criteria, such as aesthetics or egotistic motives, and prevents power plays among the family members of a child who is to be named.

- It prevents anyone from ever having to lose his or her name. Nobody's name will ever again be the compulsory consequence of whom a woman or a mother happens to be married to at the time. A person can truly and incontestably claim a name for life.

- Women will no longer have to bear the name of a former husband who is either irrelevant or despised. No one, male or female, will ever have to drag around someone else's name, or a name that clashes with one's current sense of identity.

- By linking members of the same sex, it draws on the natural, prototypical categories of male and female with which we are comfortable, because they are already deeply embedded in our imaginations.

Concerns

- What if a couple has only one child or only girls or boys?

  With the Bilineal Solution there will be families who pass only the female family name or only the male family name to future generations. All heritable naming schemes necessitate the inevitability of some family names "dying out," otherwise the names of people in future generations would be absurdly long. Under patronymy (male) family names die out all the time when a family has only girl children who marry and assume their husband's last name. The Bilineal Solution expands a family's opportunity to pass on family names since, as long as a couple has a child (of either sex) that child's name could be passed on to his or her children. Everyone has the potential— males and females—to have his or her name passed on. Systems that give parents choice over whose last name gets passed on, the mother's or the father's, like the system of alternating last names with each child, would be more prone to disintegrate and revert back to pat-ronymy. The Bilineal Solution is egalitarian in that female names and male names have equal *potential* for transmissibility.

- Why arbitrarily link the sexes, creating distinctly male and female name lines?

We're used to linking sexes, and it's already done among males with patronymy. The Bilineal Solution extends this privilege to females while not disrupting the tradition of male name lineage. Some women protest: "But I'm closer to my dad than my mom. Why should I take my mom's name?" There are lots of men who are emotionally closer to their mothers and still feel simultaneous pride in being part of a male lineage that affirms their value as a male.

- What about the desire to refer to families as unities through the use of one last name?

The Bilineal Solution encourages us to recognize both the unity and the multiplicity of families simultane-ously. It forces people to be more specific in their name references, directing their attention to everyone's distinct identity. Rather than saying "We're having the Smiths for dinner," meaning Tom Smith and whoever Mrs. Smith happens to be at the time, plus the anonymous Smith children; people will say, "Tom and Sue are coming over with their kids, Connie and Jacob."

- If you adopt a source name different from your current last name, won't it be difficult for people to acccept your new last name?

While it is true that changing last names can be hard for some people to accept, changing one's last name to a new source name is a special case. Such a change is not a matter of relabeling oneself to meet the expectations of others (as in the case, for example, of women taking husbands' last names) or of trying to project some new image to others. Rather it is a name change that reflects and affirms one's true identity by establishing a one-to-one correspondence between one's name and the inner experienced self. And people will more readily recognize and accept a sincere change that for social and personal reasons more authentically represents the person. Additionally, we have to accept that in adjusting to this new equitable system, as in all major social shifts, there will inevitably be a period of adjustment in which some pioneers will have to establish source names for themselves and their lineage, just as many blacks changed their slave names to more authentic Muslim or African names over the last few decades. The fact that some people will want and need to choose new source names, thus causing an initial adjustment period, lays the necessary naming foundation which will, in the long run, allow each person to have an unperturbed name for life.

The New Family Trees

The Bilineal Solution preserves family history in a more efficient and comprehensive way than patronymy. The Bilineal Solution simply and elegantly documents more information about families and the individuals who make them up. In so doing, we are better able to commemorate our ancestors and descendants by fixing them in our collective memory. Under the Bilineal Solution, nobody's name gets forgotten. Nobody's name is expunged from the annals of history.

Patronymy offers a crippled approach to family documentation since it could, by definition, only support patrilineal representations of families. This has had gravely deleterious effects on family history research. For instance, the early U.S. Federal Census records used to list the father as "head of the household" and then list the number of others in the family without their giving their names. Often there were people in U.S. households who didn't have the same patronymical last name as the "head of household" for any number of reasons, but genealogists have used these census records to construct patrilineal family trees. Major genealogical research errors have happened because of this.

Since children usually took their father's last name, most family trees go farther back along male lines than along female lines. At some point the researcher will encounter a woman whose maiden name isn't listed, which brings her particular line to a halt.

Unfortunately, patrilineal representations of families are necessarily *mono*lineal representations of families. Yet, this poor, limited monolineal structure was charged with the preservation of *two* kinds of family information: 1) representing kinship relationships, (who married whom, who is whose parents or children) and 2) tracing the path of a last name. A monodimensional structure cannot, by definition, express two kinds of information—paternal and maternal. It can theoretically represent either one or the other. Of course, up until now, it has only emphasized paternal information via the patronym. Conventional genealogy attempts to preserve the history of a family name *and* kinship relationships in a single lineal hierarchical form, which is conducive to a significant loss of family information and research errors.

What most people fail to realize is that a patrilineal chart reveals a minimal amount of information about families. It presents families only in terms of the issue of one man (through the device of his name). And, since patrilineal tree charts are conventionally called family trees, we are led to believe that they comprehensively represent family information, which is to say kinships as well as the path of a patronymical name. But, patrilineal family trees are structurally restricted from representing all of one's family members, because they can only accommodate family members who happen to share the name of one common male progenitor. The other family members who didn't happen to fall in the path of this name are left out of the chart.

The New Family Trees

With the Bilineal Solution one can construct trees to easily keep track of partners and siblings. The Bilineal

Solution frees patronymy of its burden, of its incompetence in comprehensively documenting family history. This new approach to family trees also plays a part in mending the deeply entrenched sexism in the field of genealogy.

The Bilineal Solution provides two kinds of family tree charts. **Kinship trees** represent relationships of consanguinity, who married whom and who begat whom. **Family name trees** trace a family name across generations. Every family will now have both patrilineal and matrilineal family name trees, resulting in the revelation and preservation of more information about families than has hitherto been preserved.

To get the idea of how these new family trees work, take a look at the Family Tree Charts at the end of this chapter. The first chart, the **kinship chart** represents three generations of progeny of the couple, Thomas Noel Lewis and Ilene Rose Summers. The kinship chart works just like the patrilineal tree charts we are accustomed to, except the family names of the children on this chart are in opposite order for girl children and boy children. The other two charts, which are **family name charts**, trace the maternal family name originating with Ilene Rose Summers and the corresponding paternal family name chart which originates with Thomas Noel Lewis.

FAMILY KINSHIP CHART

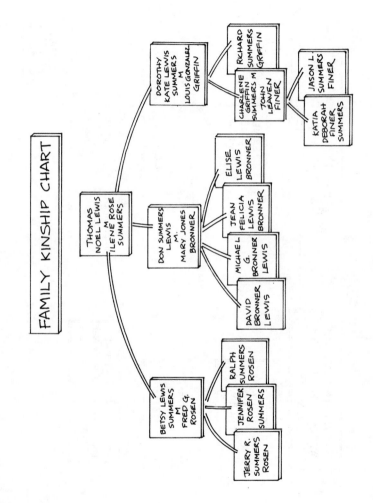

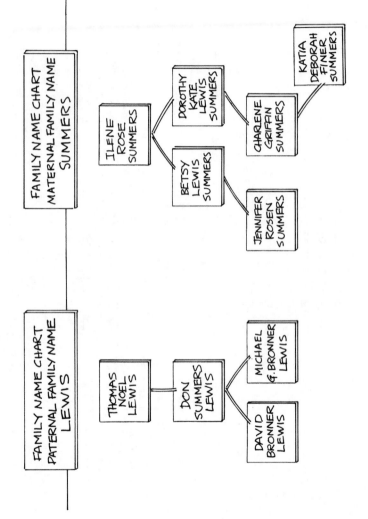

FAMILY NAME CHART
PATERNAL FAMILY NAME
LEWIS

THOMAS NOEL LEWIS

DON SUMMERS LEWIS

DAVID BRONNER LEWIS

MICHAEL G. BRONNER LEWIS

FAMILY NAME CHART
MATERNAL FAMILY NAME
SUMMERS

ILENE ROSE SUMMERS

DOROTHY KATE LEWIS SUMMERS

BETSY LEWIS SUMMERS

CHARLENE GRIFFIN SUMMERS

JENNIFER ROSEN SUMMERS

KATIA DEBORAH FINER SUMMERS

Conclusion

So entrenched is the custom of patronymy that many people— even judges, attorneys, officials, and bureaucrats who should know better—still believe that married women must take their husbands' names and children must take their fathers' names as a matter of law. This isn't true. After years of painstaking research, Una Stannard discovered that because of the *belief* that married women automatically, as a matter of law, had to take their husband's names, "special legislation is regarded as necessary in every state in order to give wives the right to retain their own name."[1]

There are statutes regarding names, but the law is not invoked unless formal disputes arise. For the most part, the law treats naming as the extra-legal, personal, familial, and emotional preserve that it is. Except when legal questions or disputes erupt about last names in relation to divorce, illegitimacy, or adoption, the law will leave average citizens alone regarding their personal naming choices.

NAMES AND THE LAW

Our present name law is very permissive in comparison to name laws of older times and the name laws that currently exist in other nations. The giving of personal names has long been regimented by laws and regulations. The first important regulation regarding personal names occurred in 1563 from the Council of Trent. As a defensive response to the growing Protestant custom of giving children the names of figures in the Old Testament or those that weren't related to Christianity at all, the Council decreed that Roman Catholic priests administering baptisms should ensure that children be given only the names of Catholic saints. This regulation is still a valid part of canon law. It was further declared that every parish must maintain meticulous registers of baptisms, including a child's name, as well as those of the child's parents and grandparents. (However, few Catholics today are aware of the rule; most feel free to name their children whatever they wish, and there is no indication that the Church objects to such freedom.) This systematic recording of names then spread among Protestants and helped cement the notion of (patronymical) last names.

In 1803, a pivotal law was passed in France, which is still on the books today, to counter the effects of the French Revolution, which allowed total naming freedom. This law restricts personal names to "names of persons known from ancient history" and "names used in various calendars." Restrictive name laws specifying the boundaries of the pool of permissible given names have been in the legal codes of the various countries of Eastern Europe.

England and the United States are practically the only countries that *in theory* adhere to the ancient Roman legal principle that everyone has the right to use and change their names as they choose as long as they aren't trying to defraud anyone. English common law has never forced married women to assume their husband's last name if they did not want to. American name law is derived from English common law, and provides that everyone may change their names for whatever reason, whenever they feel like it. Consistent with this principle is the idea that everyone, including married women, should be able to keep their last names if they want to. And even when almost all English women changed their names to their husbands' through choice, this was recognized as a custom, not as a law.

Still, even though American name law is supposed to be based on English common law, Una Stannard has demonstrated that until very recently, whenever an American woman chose not to follow custom, she was almost invariably told by members of the legal justice system and functionaries of one kind or another that her name, whether she wanted it to or not, had been automatically changed by her marriage as a matter of law. Stannard reports that it wasn't until the end of the 1960s when women started examining the whole issue of names as part of the new wave of feminism of that time, that the almost universal legal *opinion* that the law forces a wife to change her name to her husband's was challenged.

> Whereas in the 1920s the Lucy Stone League influenced a few hundred women to keep their own name, from the late 1960s to the early 1970s thousands of women from all over the country, women associated with no organization and many of whom denied they were feminists, spontaneously decided they would not take their husbands' names or would divest themselves of a husband's name they had previously taken.[2]

Stannard reports that until very recently, judges over and over expanded their jurisdiction and, going against common law, erroneously assumed it was their prerogative to tell a divorced woman whether or not she could stop using her ex-husband's name.

Internationally, there is a huge body of law that addresses what last name a woman should use when she is divorced. In

Germany, for instance, there have been laws that compel women to reassume their birth names if they are judged as the guilty party in a divorce and their former husbands wish it. Obviously these laws regard a woman's reversion to her own name as a punishment.

CHILDREN'S NAMES AND THE LAW

Name laws affecting children are nebulous. Children born to an unmarried woman may be given any last name—the mother's last name, the father's last name, or another name—and the child's name won't be disputed. According to Attorney Lombard, it isn't certain whether or not a child born to a mother who is legally married must bear its father's last name. In the case of a dispute such as when a divorced woman remarried and wanted to change her child's name to that of her present husband, judges have consistently decided in favor of the biological father providing the last name of a child. But, of course, the law has had to decide the matter only when there was a dispute. Today, most Bureaus of Records will record any last name that the parent or parents specify on the child's birth certificate.

Contradicting the common law principle that a person may be called anything he or she pleases, Lombard says

...by custom a legitimate child received his or her father's surname at birth...In the United States, a few states enacted laws which followed the common law *custom*. The vast majority of states did not resort to legislation, although apparently all states did recognize the common law *custom*.[3] [emphasis mine]

Lombard further points out that

...a good argument can be made that state statutes requiring a legitimate child to take his or her father's surname at birth are vulnerable to constitutional attack on equal protection grounds... but there is no hard case law since there have been few constitutional challenges to such statutes.[4]

...For those couples who do not wish to follow tradition, at least one influential state supreme court (the Supreme Judicial Court of Massachusetts) has held that a married couple is free to choose whatever surname they wish for their child, even if it is not either of theirs, so long as they have no fraudulent intent.[5]

...The court cited the common law principal of "freedom of choice" as well as the "private realm of family life which the state cannot enter" in support of its results.[6]

Lombard says that the real problems concerning children's last names will occur when divorced couples turn to the judicial system to solve their disputes over naming their children. She says judges will then be forced to construct a "sex neutral scheme for naming children." (The Bilineal Solution should fit the bill.)

Several people have written proposals for a Model Name Act which would address such problems. Lombard reports that one author of a draft Model Name Act "suggested that in the event of a dispute, the child should bear the surname of his similarly sexed parent..."[7]

What happens when the mother gives a child a name the father doesn't approve of? Lombard says that during the last decade, the U.S. Supreme Court has been expanding the rights of the illegitimate child as well as those of the "illegitimate father." She claims that the judicial trend is that the more the illegitimate father behaves like a legitimate father, the more likely it is that he will be treated like a legitimate father in a court of law. Behaving like a legitimate father means paying child support, spending time with the child, giving him or her gifts, and so on.

When a woman has custody of the children and wishes to change the name of the children to that of their stepfather's whose name she has adopted, the trend until now has been that judges have decided that the ex-husband has a natural right to have his children retain his name. As long as the former husband continues to pay his child support and keeps up active contact with his children, the mother can't change the children's names without his consent. But if the former husband shows signs of neglecting responsibility toward and losing interest in his children, then the mother can get the court to grant a change of name with or without his consent. Ex-husbands frequently withhold consent to such name changes, giving rise to ugly and protracted litigation.

Adopted Children

With little exception, when infants are adopted, their names are customarily changed as part of the adoption order. Most adopted children are predictably given the last name of their adoptive fathers, even though there is no explicit law compelling such a practice. Parents asking for a judge's approval of their adoption of a child may be reluctant to ask for a last name that deviates from custom, because they don't want to throw any potential snags into the adoption process. Once in a while in adoption procedures, a child will be given a hyphenated last name.

THE FORCE OF USAGE

In England and the U.S. where name laws are rooted in common law, there is little explicit legislation concerning last names for married couples and their children, because the law assumes that married women will take their husband's names and that their children will automatically have the last name of their father. And without the explicit compulsion of law, so-called illegitimate children are given their mother's last name almost universally.

That no one saw fit to legislate formally and unequivocally the principles of patronymy means there was probably little need to, for a law usually is enacted only when it is likely people will go against a principle that is held in common by a community. Since everyone more or less accepts patronymy, it doesn't need a police officer or a judge to intimidate us into conformity. Because there is a marked absence of legislation compelling patronymy, if enough of us simply ignore patronymy and put into practice the Bilineal Solution, we can undo the seeming inevitability of this patriarchal vestige.

Married women acquire their husband's name *by usage*, by the same usage principle that applies when the Richards, Williams, and Patricias of the world become known as Dick, Bill, and Patty. No statute compels women to change their names at marriage. If brides simply don't start using their husbands' names and keep their own name on all their records, the law will stay out of their affairs. As California attorneys David Ventura Loeb and David W. Brown advise, "Don't go around voluntarily telling people you got married just so you can tell them not to change your records. You will only be creating problems for yourself." Similarly, if couples adopt the Bilineal Solution for their children and don't fight about it, the law will leave them alone. In adopting the Bilineal Solution for children, couples are probably shaping future law regarding children's names. Name law for children is so inchoate right now, it is susceptible to being changed by our customs, which are moving in a more progressive and egalitarian direction.

In any considered discussion of names, inevitably people ask whether the law will permit the adoption of the Bilineal Solution. People express concern that if they go against patronymy, they will be forced to deal with some complicated, and perhaps expensive, legal process to change or keep their names.

The most effective way of establishing the name by which you wish to be known has nothing to do with the law or bureaucratic proceedings. The law is really rather impotent when it comes to enforcing the use of a particular name or enjoining someone from using a particular name if he or she is an ordinary person not wishing to defraud someone. To put people on notice as to what your name is, whether you are changing your name, or retaining it upon marriage, or bestowing a counter-conventional name on your child, exploit the ordinary minutiae of your life as a vehicle of announcement. For instance, the way you write or print your return address on envelopes signals how you wish to be addressed. On your mailbox post all relevant names exactly as you wish them to be remembered.

If you are establishing a new source name, change your name on your driver's license first. This is easy to do, and most other agencies will recognize the authority of whatever name is printed on your license. Next, get your bank checks written with your new name as this is one of the best ways to proclaim and establish your name. Checks have an official aura, so every time you pass one to a merchant, friend, or relative, the receiver is reinforced in the habit of referring to you by the name you wish. A check has much more durable and manipulative force than say, the more official change one might get through formal channels on a passport, for instance.

Patronymy thrives because men, women, and children follow the patronymical naming system. There is, for instance, a widespread erroneous notion that marriage certificates (or some fictitious document) lawfully change women's names. Women's names are changed when they marry because women themselves change them through use. They respond to people who call them Mrs. So-and-So, and as soon as they return from their honeymoon, they usually march over to department stores, banks, motor vehicle departments, passport offices, and so on to inform these agencies that they have changed their name since their marriage.

You don't have to bother with the law at all when it comes to adopting the Bilineal Solution, unless, in so doing, you anticipate some kind of legal dispute. The legal mechanics of how to change names vary from state to state. In California, where the name laws are similar to those in other states, people legally change their names through usage. If you anticipate child custody questions, you must know your state's procedures, case precedents and practices, and there's a good chance you'll need a lawyer.

How to Establish a New Source Name

One of the greatest benefits of the Bilineal Solution is that no one ever has to undergo a socially compelled name change that could undermine one's sense of identity. There are those, on the other hand, who will consciously choose to change their names to affirm their identity through the adoption of a new source name. If you want to establish a source name, you should have the name change recorded on the following:

- Bank accounts

- Driver's license

- Social Security card

- Car registration

- All credit cards

- Voter registration

- Welfare payments

- Passports

- Property deeds

- Mortgages and loans

- Wills

- Life and health insurance policies

- Post office records

- Telephone listing

- School records

- Stocks and bonds

- Other official documents

- Library cards

- Memberships (professional associations, community centers, clubs, and so forth)

In establishing a source name you may have to be tough on occasion with bureaucrats, who can be obtuse or mean-spirited with those who don't follow custom. When dealing with an intractable official or clerk, be armed with the facts of the pertinent name law of your state and insist on your name rights. When you change your name by usage in the absence of petitioning the court, it is often a good idea to write up an official-looking proclamation of your legal name change. Just write a statement declaring your current name, and that you are changing your name to xyz. State that you have no intention of defrauding anyone with the name change. You might get this statement notarized. Laser printing this document is a good idea as this is a cheap way of making documents appear official.[8] You can get your document laser printed at a local computer service bureau or deluxe photo-copy service in any urban center. Keep in mind, this document isn't legally or officially necessary; it just might make your life a little easier.

Some women who read this book will be inspired to change their names (women who took their husbands' name at marriage, or women who want to change their name to start a female lineage per the Bilineal Solution). Most of these name changes can be established by usage in extra-legal ways.

To gain legal recognition of a new name, the main thing is to be consistent in your use of your new name. Use it all the time, in all situations. In California, for instance, people who use new names in only parts of their lives have not legally changed their names. *Nom de plumes* or stage names, for example, are not considered legally changed names. You are going to have to contact all of the organizations with which you have dealings and inform them of your name change. You have to tell all your friends and family members about your new name, and you should introduce yourself to new acquaintances by your new name. Almost all government agencies will now accept a change of name simply through usage. The passport office is the only agency that is notorious for being difficult in connection with name changes, but don't be discouraged; just check their current procedures. Because under patronymy, women routinely change their names, the Passport Office (and other official agencies) are used to dealing with name changes and have to accommodate all legitimate (i.e., non-fraudulent) requests.

Changing a minor child's name who has a patronymical last name, even in accordance with the Bilineal Solution, is unethical. That is tampering with a child's developing identity. Given everything I've said in this book so far about the power of names and their bearing on the construction of self, it's not proper for adults to impose naming principles on their already named children. What a child has been named and called should be treated as accomplished fact. There should be no pressure, no browbeating; the choice should be left up to children to call themselves what they wish when the appropriate time comes.

WHAT REALLY STANDS IN OUR WAY?

If the law doesn't present the obstacles to name change, what stands in our way of putting compulsory patronymy to rest at last? "Today's treason is tomorrow's orthodoxy," declared Doris Lessing. The Bilineal Solution will be regarded as treason for some time. But rather than the anticipated thicket of legal obstructions, we find that the real challenges that lie ahead are in people's attitudes and their corresponding behavior.

It's very hard to challenge entrenched social practices.

Patronymy got here before the Bilineal Solution. The topic of names and the prospect of changing the way our society encodes them is extremely threatening to the social order. But, as with all major social change, a new idea starts out as a minority viewpoint, and gains acceptance gradually as it wins converts over from the prevailing view. In order for there to be real and lasting change in how our society names individuals, a large number of people have to change themselves; they have to adopt an unconventional naming strategy in the face of great opposition.

Emotional barriers to change are very difficult to surmount with reason. There are so many customs to which generally sensible people adhere, which on scrutiny are at best silly and at worst dangerous. Most people can be intellectually convinced that it's silly or dangerous to wear clothing that is uncomfortable, such as high heels, but perfectly "rational" people do. A man with only the barest acquaintance with logic can be intellectually persuaded that men could benefit from wearing skirts or carrying purses, but that same man is not going to don a dress or a purse. Similarly, you can demonstrate to "reasonable" people that male circumcision is medically unnecessary and hurts babies but these same people will nevertheless choose to have their child circumcised, even for nonreligious reasons.

How do we change people, more importantly, change ourselves, when it turns out that most people aren't as reasonable as they'd like to think? We need a small, but fiercely dedicated group of naming pioneers to flaunt convention. They draw attention to the absurdity and arbitrariness of patronymy, and they will probably endure censure. But like the suffragists and the first women who dared to keep their own names, these people will, by their individual choices and behavior, establish a climate of increased permissibility that will make it safe for others. Una Stannard reminds us that "Before 1921 the majority of women did NOT want to vote; it was a tiny minority, willing to endure the hostility of society, who gave women a right they now take for granted."[9] So it will be with a woman's right to have a name of her own and to pass that name on to her children.

CAN INDIVIDUALS REALLY CHANGE?

Can we really make significant changes in the way we name? There are actually two parts to this question. Can we as individuals change, and can the people around us change? Una Stannard reminds us that, even after a resurgence of feminism, 99 percent of American women still take their husband's name at marriage. It follows from that statistic that children will continue to be given their father's last name, for changing how children are named is the more radical move. Therefore, the primary responsibility for the first step toward change rests with women. Men generally don't care about names, unless their privilege is directly challenged. So they are not as a group naturally motivated to instigate change. When women stop taking their husband's names, a dissonance is created in the representational structure of the marriage. People feel uncomfortable when parents have different last names from their children. As more and more women keep their names for life, the dissonance will increasingly intrude into individual relationships and our collective mode of representing families. Even women who vocally disavow any association with things feminist will feel the dissonance and feel a need to do something about it. Even men who have a vested interest in preserving the implied privilege and superiority that patronymy proclaims, will have to feel the dissonance, because they will be marrying women who will no longer docilely give over their identities in name. Then compulsive patronymy as it applies to children will be rendered subject to question, and more and more people will respond by changing the way they name their children.

One of the more overwhelming obstacles to our changing as individuals with respect to names has to do with how women think and feel about themselves as a result of the fundamental posture from which they have been conditioned to face the world: a relational and adaptive posture. There are arguably many benefits of this flexible existential posture as contrasted with the dualistic, inflexible I/other posture which men are conventionally taught to adopt. Books are being written, seminars are being given, whole theories are being built on the dangers of the extremes of the I/other posture. It is no exaggeration to say that a relational posture, a way of being that is naturally, instinctively accommodating and inclusive of other human beings, other life forms, and of nature, is what keeps our planet glued together. Yet women have been unwittingly sentenced by their posture to a life of existential derivation and dependence, a tendency to look outside themselves for confirmation of their very is-ness and who-ness. This fundamental existential uncertainty is intrinsic to the way we are named and willingly permit ourselves to be named.

We tend to overlook that when a woman gets married and changes her name, there is a very active dimension in her role in the name change. While it is true that her change of name conforms to expectation, she nevertheless has to go out actively to various agencies and organizations, fill out tons of forms, and set into motion the apparatus of name change. Similarly, when a woman has a baby at a hospital, as most women do, it is usually she who has the principal contact with the birth certificate representative who will inscribe in the public record the newborn's name. Women are the active agents of patronymy. Mothers formally give their children the fathers' last names; mothers sign the name documents. Why do they do this? No one is physically or overtly forced to put a baby's father's last name on the name document.

Women are so programmed into being relational, they are uncomfortable bearing a name different from their husband's and even more uncomfortable giving their children names other than that of the children's father's. We still, even the strongest among us, want to grow up, and in some sense, be taken under big daddy's wing and be protected from that cold cruel world, and many of us are terrified of other people's judgments about our choices. This is the condition that has to be changed.

The prevalent naming pattern of a culture evolves in response to the changing social mores of that culture. So, just as it was standard in England and later America, for women to be known as Mrs. John Jones,[10] this changed— among certain social groups—when it became no longer acceptable to women to be referred to as if they didn't even have claim to their own first names.

As our culture changes, representatives of the new way will inaugurate the signs of the new order (whether it's fashion, language, art, architecture, or name changes). These brave pioneers may at first be perceived as isolated freaks. They may be condemned for their apparent extremity, but every culture relies on these brave souls to expand the boundaries of permissibility for everyone else. Doris Lessing said:

> ...[I]t is my belief that it is always the individual, in the long run, who will set the tone, provide the real development in a society.

It is not always easy to go on valuing the individual, when everywhere individuals are so put down, denigrated, swamped by mass thinking, mass movements and, on a smaller scale, by the group.

It is particularly hard for young people, faced with what seem like impervious walls of obstacles, to have belief in their ability to change things, to keep their personal and individual viewpoints intact. I remember very clearly how it seemed to me in my late teens and early twenties, seeing only what seemed to be impregnable systems of thought, of belief—governments that seemed unshakable...

Looking back now, I no longer see these enormous blocs, nations, movements, systems, faiths, religions, but only individuals, people who when I was young I might have valued, but not with much belief in the possibility of their changing anything. Looking back, I see what a great influence an individual may have, even an apparently obscure person, living a small, quiet life. It is individuals who change societies, give birth to ideas, who, standing out against tides of opinion, change them...[11]

Though most people's imaginations have been crippled by the force of precedent, women who keep their own names are becoming less and less freakish in the public eye as more and more women are refusing to be nominally in a man's shadow. How quickly we forget that not too long ago, it was very difficult for women just to keep their own last names at marriage.

As for children's names, we are still at the stage in which people who confer an unconventional name on their child will be thought freakish. These so called freaks will soon be labeled as "feminists." While in many eyes, the label "feminist" is derogatory, someone who is feminist is not an isolated freak but rather a legitimate member of an established group that is reported about in the news. Finally, the new naming customs will be normalized in the public imagination. This was the evolutionary pattern with the increasing acceptance of Ms. as a form of address. First a few isolated women insisted on it and were treated like mutants from outer space; then the use of Ms. accorded you *ipso facto* membership in the class of people known as feminists; eventually it became accepted and normalized, not the standard, but perfectly acceptable.

It turns out that for most people contemplating a name change, the people who are most obstructive are those who are related to you. While fathers are often secretly happy that a daughter chooses to keep her name when she marries, husbands and husband's parents are often not at all thrilled that a woman won't take her husband's name, and, worst of all, when a child is not given the father's name. Your family members and supposed friends can make it hellish for you. They won't address letters to you or your children with the correct names. They won't introduce you by your right name. Or they will hector you by saying "And I'd like you to meet...now what are you calling yourself these days, Dear?" You will be pigeon-holed as a trouble-maker, a fanciful rebel.

As difficult as it is to weather all of the harassment, especially when it comes from your own kin or people whose opinion really matters, we have to understand how our choice affects these people. We have to be sensitive to the feelings of others. What we are doing by tampering with the sacred cow of names is literally changing the world. People sense this; they know it. And they're very threatened by it.

FEAR OF THE STIGMA OF ILLEGITIMACY OR "THE BROKEN HOME"

One fear, whether acknowledged or not, among those who are close to you is the fear that a child who bears a nontraditional name, a girl bearing her mother's last name, for example, will be perceived as illegitimate. This concern arises out of a willingness to accept patronymy's rules for encoding names as the standard. Within patronymy, children with their mother's last names are illegitimate and that notion bears with it a great burden. Nobody wishes to pass on such a burden to a child, so there is a quite sincere protectionist impulse in operation here. But there is also a craven unwillingness to shift codes, an unwillingness to stop turning to patronymy's authority as *the* naming code.

It is often said in discussions of naming alternatives for children that it isn't fair to children to give them names other than their fathers', because they will be taunted. Other children will think there is something the matter with them and their families. There will be an implication that the child's mother has had at least a couple of marriages, or that she had the child out of wedlock.

What appears to be true is that kids don't really care about what other kids are named (unless it's a funny sounding name, in which case they will show a child no mercy). At the most, they might ask a girl why she has a different name from her father, and she quite naturally would reply that that was the name she was given. Period. Children are not concerned about the artificial stigma fostered by tired religious notions regarding legitimacy. They don't even know what legitimacy is, and they don't care. They are attached to their names, whatever they are, and they expect others to be similarly attached.

In fact, by providing that children receive their opposite-sex parent's last name as a middle name, the Bilineal Solution does mitigate the perception of illegitimacy and clearly announces a child's relationship to its parent of the opposite sex. And, of course, now that more and more women are keeping their last names at marriage, we already have the increasingly common phenomenon of a mother with a last name different from her children. Why not go all the way and have girls share their mothers' last names, with their fathers' last names as middle names, and boys similarly share their fathers' last names, with their mothers' last names as middle names? It's not really that big a leap to make, since under patronymy parents already expect their daughters to end up with a different last name from their father's (at marriage). And with the Bilineal Solution, the fathers preserve the opportunity to pass their name down through generations of their sons.

Some protest that you can't "intentionally engineer naming custom." This really isn't a question of engineering, but a shift of consensus. And shifts of consensus are, of course, possible; in fact, they happen every day. Nothing would ever change if there weren't regular daily shifts in consensus. Consensus shifts when individuals change, when we change our feelings about the worth of women and our own resistance to change.

THE HABIT OF PATRONYMY

One of the biggest obstructions to change over from patronymy is that, irrespective of its implied politics, it's a habit. And it's a habit that is self-validated and self-perpetuated by ignorance of the law and the seeming immutability of custom. Even those people who have the best of intentions will not always remember to honor your name choices. A very close friend and colleague who is well acquainted with my position on names actually finished a conversation we had been having about this book by asking me if I'd like to come to dinner with my family at his home. We agreed on a date, and he called out to his wife "The Loudons will be coming for dinner on the 13th. Okay, Sue?" My last name is not Loudon, neither of my daughters' last names is Loudon. I am married to a John Loudon. When Frank returned his attention to our phone call, he didn't even realize his mistake; it was reflexive.

UNVEILING YOUR NEW NAME OR AFFIRMING THE ONE YOU'VE GOT

You can be creative and have fun with your name change. If you are changing your name, you can do as a friend of mine did. To celebrate her adoption of her mother's maiden name as her source name, she threw a name unveiling party to mark the change and to guard against her having to make tiresome explanations to friends and family. All her loved ones came over to celebrate, and she formally announced her new name. The spirit of the occasion was joyous as she embraced her new name with firm resolve. When she marries, she's going to keep her name, and she'll pass her name on to her female children.

Naming rituals (which are as fundamental in other cultures as celebrations of wedding anniversaries are in our culture) can be a very meaningful way of formally claiming a new name or affirming the name you have. A journalist recently had a naming ritual when she changed her name to one that seemed more fitting than her birth name. Her birth name was Teresa Cross (Terry) and she decided to establish the matrilineal source name, Berns, her mother's "maiden" name. She invited her mother and several very close women friends to enact her naming ritual. The group gathered in a circle to say good-bye to her former name. Terry told the group what was special about her birth name and what it represented to her. Then she thanked her name/former self for all the riches it had brought to her life. Next, everyone welcomed her new name and intoned it several times saying, "You are now Terry Berns." Terry's mother told a moving story about what Terry's birth name meant to her and vividly described the unsung personalities in Terry's maternal background. Then they celebrated the rest of the evening.

I envision a time soon when there will be name jamborees: gatherings where women, men, and children get together to declare and celebrate newly chosen names or to affirm the birth name they were given. There could be workshops on matronymic genealogies, history of women's names, the future of women's and children's names.

STOP "DOING" PATRONYMY

While supplanting patronymy with something else does not eliminate male power and privilege, establishing the Bilineal Solution erodes the automatic acceptance of male primacy. When we stop following the custom of patronymy, we can daily reinforce an experience of ourselves outside of patriarchal definitions. Dale Spender points out that just as consciousness-raising "does not remove males from the influential positions in society nor does it provide women with equitable wages...[T]here is a consensus which must accompany power and at the moment too many people are content to see male power and dominance as reasonable and natural."[12]

To undo patronymy, you must enact a naming scheme for yourself and your family that produces names that feel right for everyone involved. It means withdrawing your support of patronymical representations of yourself or your family. For example, if you receive junk mail addressed to "Mrs. + your husband's name," dump it in the trash. The problem of patronymy will be solved, not by a spate of clever solutions, but by a dedicated and considered choice to not do it anymore, and to courageously enact a new way of naming, the Bilineal Solution.

The real solution to patronymy is simply to STOP DOING IT. Name yourself and your children consciously, with conviction. Don't get lost in the labyrinth of batting around candidates for the best alternative naming solution. Remember what the goal is: The overcoming of the perception, which is reinforced through patronymy, that men are better than women. The most powerful antidote to this noxious perception is to follow the Bilineal Solution.

This is a means of revolt and revolution that doesn't involve violence; it's not illegal, and you don't even have to become a member of an organization to participate. All you have to do is establish and keep your name for the rest of your life and, if you have children, pass your name on to them, thereby contributing to the creation of a more equitable world for them to grow up in. You can, in this small way, withdraw consensus to the primacy, centrality, and supremacy of males. Through the way we name ourselves and our childen, we can stop substantiating male entitlement at female expense.

Naming ourselves using the Bilineal Solution is a way of altering perception that is so subtle, its colossal radical nature and effects are easily underestimated. Yet the mightiest revolutions are revolutions in perception, which then prompt change in our beliefs and actions. As we name ourselves differently, we change how we perceive and value males and females and how we construct the self, our selves, our world: I, Me, Us. We. We can represent males and females in a way that reflects their truly equal human value. So, let's do it.

Notes

The Power and Peril of Our Last Names

1. Dale Spender, *Man Made Language* (London: Routledge & Kegan Paul, 1980), 4.
2. *Ibid.*, 90-91.
3. *Ibid.*, 3.
4. Arthur Kurzweil, *From Generation to Generation* (New York: Schocken Books, 1982), 35-36.
5. Dale Spender, *Man Made Language* (London: Routledge & Kegan Paul, 1980), 25.
6. Arthur Kurzweil, *From Generation to Generation* (New York: Schocken Books, 1982), 27.
7. Anna Quindlen, "My Name and I," *The New York Times*, 19 June 1987.

Why Patronymy Persists

1. Dale Spender, *Man Made Language* (London: Routledge & Kegan Paul, 1980), 2.
2. H. D. Krause, *Illegitimacy: Law and Social Policy* 32-33 (1971), as cited in Frederica K. Lombard, "The Law on Naming Children: Past, Present and Occasionally Future," *Names* 32, no. 2 (June 1984).

A Brief History of Patronymy

1. H. L. Mencken, *Supplement Two: The American Language* (New York: Alfred A. Knopf, 1962), 430-431.
2. Letter from Una Stannard, November 27, 1987. Please read chapter 19, The Mother of Us All" in Una Stannard, *Mrs. Man* (San Francisco: GERMAINBOOKS, 1977), for her full argument.

Different Ways of Naming Ourselves

1. Frederica K. Lombard, "The Law on Naming Children: Past, Present and Occasionally Future," *Names* 32, no. 2 (June 1984).
2. Gloria Steinem, "Looking to the Future," *Ms.* Magazine, July/August 1987, 57.

Conclusion

1. Una Stannard, *Married Women v. Husband's Names: The Case for Wives who Keep Their Own Names* (San Francisco: GERMAINBOOKS, 1973), 37.
2. Una Stannard, "Manners Make Laws: Married Women's Names in the United States." *Names* 32, no. 2 (June 1984).
3. Frederica K. Lombard, "The Law on Naming Children: Past, Present and Occasionally Future," *Names* 32, no. 2 (June 1984).
4. *Ibid.*
5. Secretary of the Commonwealth v. City Clerk, 373 Mass. 178, 366 N.E. 2d 139 (1974) as quoted in Frederica K. Lombard, "The Law on Naming Children: Past, Present

and Occasionally Future," *Names* 32, no. 2 (June 1984).

6. *Idem.* at 185, 366 N.E. 2d at 723 as quoted in Frederica K. Lombard, "The Law on Naming Children: Past, Present and Occasionally Future," *Names* 32, no. 2 (June 1984).

7. Dannin, "Proposal for a Model Name Act", *10 U. of Mich. J. of Law Reform* 153, 173-74 (1976) as quoted in Frederica K. Lombard, "The Law on Naming Children: Past, Present and Occasionally Future," *Names* 32, no. 2 (June 1984).

8. For a good example of the wording of a written declaration of legal name change, see David Ventura Loeb and David W. Brown, *How to Change Your Name* (Berkeley, California: Nolo Press, 1986).

9. Una Stannard, *Mrs. Man* (San Francisco: GERMAIN-BOOKS, 1977).

10. For more information about this custom, see Una Stannard, *Mrs. Man* (San Francisco: GERMAINBOOKS, 1977).

11. Doris Lessing, *Prisons We Choose To Live Inside* (New York: Harper and Row, Publishers, 1987), 72-73.

12. Dale Spender, *Man Made Language* (London: Routledge & Kegan Paul, 1980), 5.